*The Worst
of
Truly Tasteless
Jokes*

The Worst
of
Truly Tasteless
Jokes

Blanche Knott

St. Martin's Press
New York

THE WORST OF TRULY TASTELESS JOKES. Copyright © 1986 by Blanche Knott. All rights reserved. Printed in the United States of America. No part of this book may be used or reproduced in any manner whatsoever without written permission except in the case of brief quotations embodied in critical articles or reviews. For information, address St. Martin's Press, 175 Fifth Avenue, New York, N.Y. 10010.

Typeset by Fisher Composition, Inc.

Library of Congress Cataloging in Publication Data

Knott, Blanche.
  The worst of truly tasteless jokes.

  Selected jokes from the author's: Truly tasteless jokes, Truly tasteless jokes two, and Truly tasteless jokes three.
    1. American wit and humor. I. Title.
PN6162.K62 1986   818'.5402   86-13067
ISBN 0-312-892918

First Edition

10 9 8 7 6 5

For Morgan
—she had to find out sometime

Contents

Polish

Why don't Polish women use vibrators?
They chip their teeth.

□   □   □

A Polish guy came home early from work to find his
wife lying on the bed, panting and sweaty. "Honey, I
think I'm having a heart attack," she gasped. The Pole
ran downstairs to call the doctor, and on the way his
little son told him, "Daddy, daddy, there's a naked man
in the closet."

The Pole ran back upstairs, opened the closet,
pulled out his best friend, and yelled, "Jesus, Jerry,
Marie's having a heart attack and here you are, scaring
the kids!"

□   □   □

Then there were the two Poles speeding down the highway at 100 mph. "Hey," asked the driver, "see any cops
following us?"

"Yup."

"Shit. Are his flashers on?"

His passenger turned back, thought it over, and answered, "Yup . . . nope . . . yup . . . nope . . . yup. . . ."

□   □   □

A Polish couple and a single man are shipwrecked on a desert island. It doesn't take long for the single guy to get pretty horny, and finally he comes up with an idea for getting into the wife's pants. Climbing way up a tall palm tree, he hollers back down to the couple, "Hey y'all, quit fucking down there!" The Pole looks over at his wife—who's standing ten feet away—and says, "What the hell's he talking about?"

This goes on for several hours, until the married man is overcome with curiosity and decides to climb up the palm to see for himself what the other guy's problem is. As he's going up, the horny fellow jumps down to the beach, grabs the wife, and proceeds to screw her like crazy.

The Pole finally reaches the top where the single guy had been, looks down, and says, "Goddamn if he wasn't right—it does look like they're fucking down there!"

□   □   □

A young Polish girl was hitchhiking along the Interstate, and a big semi pulled over to pick her up. The driver was a serious CB addict, and the dashboard boasted an enormous CB radio.

"That's the best radio ever made," he explained to

the bug-eyed girl. "You can talk anywhere in the *world* with it."

"No kidding," she gasped. "Boy, I would really love to talk to my mother in Poland."

"Oh, yeah?"

"I would give anything to talk to my mother in Poland."

"*Anything?*" he asked.

"Anything," she assured him.

"Well, maybe we can work something out," he leered, pulling his cock, by this time erect, out of his pants.

So the girl leaned over, bent down, and said loudly, "HELLO, MOM?"

□   □   □

Did you hear about the Polish bulletproof vest?

You get your money back if it doesn't work right.

□   □   □

Two Poles went deer hunting and managed to shoot a big buck. Each grabbed a hind leg and they were pulling it through the woods when they happened across a game warden. After making sure their hunting licenses were in order, the warden said, "If you don't mind a suggestion, fellas, you'll have an easier time pulling that deer along if you hold it by the antlers instead of the feet."

The Poles decided he probably knew what he was talking about, so they each took hold of an antler and started off again. "He was right," commented one a few minutes later, "this really is easier."

"Yeah," said his buddy, "but we're getting farther from the truck."

□ □ □

A Polish family is sitting around watching TV and the father leans over to the mother and says, "Let's send the kids to the S-H-O-W so we can fuck."

□ □ □

An American tourist was visiting the town in Poland from which his grandparents had emigrated when he saw a big crowd by the side of the road. Curiosity got the better of him and he stopped to ask an onlooker what was going on. The fellow explained that a protester against the repression of Polish civil liberties had doused himself with gasoline and set himself on fire. "That's terrible," gasped the American. "But why is everyone still standing around?"

"Someone's taking a collection for his wife and kids," the man explained. "Would you be willing to help?"

"Well, sure," said the tourist. "I suppose I could spare a gallon or two."

□ □ □

Why don't Polish women breast-feed their babies?
It hurts too much when they boil the nipples.

□ □ □

A Pole is walking down the street and passes a hardware store advertising a sale on a chainsaw that is capable of cutting 700 trees in seven hours. The Pole thinks that's a great deal and decides to buy one.

The next day, he comes back with the saw and complains to the salesman that the thing didn't come close to chopping down the 700 trees the ad said it would.

"Well," said the salesman, "let's test it out back."

Finding a log, the salesman pulls the starter cord and the saw makes a great roaring sound.

"What's that noise?" asks the Pole.

□   □   □

How can you tell the Polish secretary?

She's the one with White-Out all over her computer screen.

□   □   □

A Polish man made the acquaintance of a young woman in a bar, and she accepted his invitation to come back to his apartment. After a few drinks and some soft music the Pole suggested retiring to the bedroom, and the young woman was willing. Soon they were going at it hot and heavy.

Right in the middle of everything the Pole stopped dead, looked at her, and said, "Hey, you don't have herpes, do you?"

"NO!" she said. "Why would you ask that?"

"That's a relief," said the Pole. "The last girl didn't tell me until it was too late."

□   □   □

How about the Pole who was sent up into space with a monkey? The first day, a red light went on and the monkey took down all the instrument readings. The second day, a red light went on and the monkey took out his slide rule and made all the appropriate calculations. The third day, a green light went on.

"What do I do now?" asked the Pole.

"Feed the monkey," said a little voice from Earth.

□ □ □

Did you hear about the Polish gynecologist who used two fingers?

He wanted a second opinion.

□ □ □

A Pole was working at a construction site where the boss left each day at 11:00 AM and was gone for two hours. This became such a regular occurrence that the rest of the workers decided to spend the two hours in the bar across the street, but the Pole decided to head home for some extra nookie with his wife. When he arrived home, he found his boss busy banging his wife in the bedroom! Well, he walked right out and headed back to the job.

The following day the Pole was working his ass off when everyone headed across to the bar. "Hey, Ski, aren't you coming?" asked one of them.

"Hell, no," said the Pole. "I almost got caught yesterday!"

□ □ □

How many Poles does it take to start a car?

Five. One to steer, one to work the pedals, two to

push, and one to sit under the hood saying "Va-room, va-room."

□   □   □

One day, while walking down the street, a Pole stops to ask a man what time it is. "It's three o'clock" is the polite reply.

"Thank you," says the Pole. "It's funny, but I've been asking that question all day long and each time I get a different answer."

□   □   □

Did you hear about the old Polish man who told his children that his only wish was to be buried at sea?

His two sons drowned digging his grave.

□   □   □

A Pole makes a doctor's appointment because his hemorrhoids are really bothering him. The doctor gives him some suppositories and tells him to come back in a week for a checkup. "How's it going?" he asks the patient a week later.

"I gotta tell you the truth, Doc," said the Pole. "For all the good these pills did me, I coulda shoved them up my ass."

□   □   □

Hear about the Pole who lost $50 on the football game?

$25 on the game and $25 on the instant replay.

A Pole was jumped by two muggers and fought like hell, but he was finally subdued. His attackers went through his pockets. "You mean you fought like that for fifty-seven cents?" asked one of the muggers incredulously.

"That's all you wanted?" moaned the Pole. "I thought you were after the four hundred dollars in my shoe."

□ □ □

What did the Pole do when the doctor found sugar in his urine?

He pissed on his corn flakes.

□ □ □

After World War Two, two Poles return to their destroyed village to locate the first one's wife. Going through the rubble, Victor comes across a dismembered arm and calls over, "Hey, Stanley, wasn't this Anya's arm? I think it's the wristwatch you gave her."

"I dunno, Victor," says Stanley, and they walk on. A little farther on, Victor comes across a severed leg. "Stanley, couldn't this be part of Anya? She had great legs."

Stanley shrugs and they walk on. Finally the energetic Victor comes across a woman's head, which he holds out at arms' length for his friend's inspection.

"Nope," says Stanley at last. "Anya was much taller."

The Polish couple asked their kid what he wanted for his birthday. He said, "I wanna watch." So they let him.

□　　□　　□

A 6′ 8″, 280-pound black man walked into a bar, sat down next to a white guy, and said, "I's big and I's black and I loves to fuck white women!" The guy was so terrified that he put down his beer and ran out of the bar.

The black moved over next to another white man and said, "I's big and I's black and I just loves to fuck white women." The white guy took one look at him, blanched, and ran out of the bar.

The black then went over to a Pole who was having a few at the bar and said, "I's big and I's black and I *loves* to fuck white women."

The Pole looked at him and said, "I don't blame you one bit. I wouldn't fuck a nigger either."

□　　□　　□

Did you hear the two biggest Polish lies?
　1) The check is in my mouth.
　2) I won't come in your mail.

Black

What do you call a black man on a Palomino horse?
Leroy Rogers.

□   □   □

Finding out that Alabama was starting up a hunting season on blacks, a young redneck rushed to obtain a license and to stock up on shells. Soon he was riding down a country road where he came across a whole bunch of blacks picking watermelons in a field. Screeching to a halt, he opened fire, only to be promptly accosted by a game warden who shouted, "What the hell do you think you're doing?"

"I got a license, right here," protested the sportsman.

"Maybe so," countered the official, "but not to hunt in a baited field."

□   □   □

Why did God give black men such huge pricks?
Because he was so sorry about what he'd done to their hair.

□   □   □

This big black guy is in the Cadillac showroom eyeballing the most deluxe model, and over his face comes a grin that just won't quit. Perplexed, the car salesman comes up to him and asks, "Excuse me, sir, but are you thinking of buying that car?"

"I ain't thinking about buying that car," came the answer. "I is *gonna* buy that car."

"Very good, sir. But that car's very expensive—why are you smiling so much?"

"Cause I'm thinkin' about pussy!"

□   □   □

This black man was down on his luck, sitting on a curb in skid row slugging the last of his Thunderbird, when an angel appeared next to him. Saying how sorry she felt for him, she asked about his life and found out Sam had been a window washer, and a pretty good window washer at that.

"Well why don't you go to L.A.," suggested the angel, "and see if you can't land a job window-washing on some of those skyscrapers out there?"

This struck Sam as a pretty good idea so he cleaned up his act, hitched a ride to California, landed a job and was doing fine, when one day the angel materialized on the thirty-ninth floor window ledge right next to him. "So do you believe in angels now?" she asked sweetly.

"I sure do," answered the window washer.

"And would you put all your trust in God?"

"You bet," said Sam.

"And if you undid your harness and leaned back off the ledge, do you think God would hold you safe?" asked the angel. Sam nodded confidently, undid his harness, and fell thirty-nine stories—SPLAT!—to the sidewalk.

The little angel shook her head, looked up at the sky, and murmured, "Lord, I just don't see how I ever made it into heaven, hating black folks the way I do. . . ."

□ □ □

This black guy walks into a bar with a beautiful parrot on his shoulder.

"Wow!" says the bartender. "That is really something. Where'd you get it?"

"Africa," says the parrot.

□ □ □

Did you hear about the new perfume for black women? It's called Eau-de-doo-dah-day.

□ □ □

After the War, a Yankee general bought himself a plantation down South which he really loved. Every Saturday night he'd throw a big party for his Southern friends, but somebody would always yell out "Damn Yankee" at some point, and this really upset the general. Finally, a friend confided in him that people would stop calling him a damn Yankee if he'd make love to a black girl.

So the very next day he went down to the colored part of town, found himself an attractive black girl, and they went to bed. In the heat of their lovemaking, she screamed, "Ooh, you damn Yankee!"

The furious general stopped midstroke and demanded to know how she knew he was a Yankee.

Smiling winsomely, she said, "'Cause dem Southern boys don't kiss me like you do."

□ □ □

What do you call a black hitchhiker?
Stranded.

□ □ □

A white man walks into a bar wearing a button that says, "I hate niggers" and sits down at the bar.

"Listen buddy, some people here won't appreciate that button. You'd better take it off," the bartender warns.

"I don't care," says the man. "I hate niggers. They're dumb, stupid and smelly. I just hate 'em."

Shaking his head, the bartender goes to serve another customer. Five minutes later, a big black man walks in and sits down next to the man with the button.

"Hey," the black man says, spying the button for the first time, "I don't like that. Take it off or I'll take it off for you."

"Hell no," replies the white man, "I hate niggers. They're dumb and stupid. I hate them."

"Then I'll just have to remove it for you," counters the black man, "Let's go outside."

Both men go out to the alley behind the bar and the black whips out a huge switchblade.

"See, *see* how stupid you niggers are," the white man chuckles, "bringing a knife to a gunfight."

The NAACP sent an agent to Alabama to check the progress in integration of churches. After a few weeks of checking around, he called headquarters to file his report. "How about the Catholics?" asks his boss.

"The Catholics are doing okay; they got the right idea."

"What about the Methodists?"

"They've come a long way," says the agent. "They're doing just fine."

"And the Baptists?" asks the boss.

"I just want to know one thing—when they baptize you, how long are they supposed to hold you under?"

□ □ □

Did you hear about the new black French restaurant? Chez What?

□ □ □

What did the southern governor say about the holiday for Martin Luther King?

"Shoot four more and we'll take a week off."

□ □ □

A fisherman from Maine went to Alabama on his vacation. He rented a boat, rowed out to the middle of the lake, and cast his line, but when he looked down into the water he was horrified to see a black man wrapped in chains lying on the bottom of the lake. He quickly rowed to shore and ran to the police station. "Sheriff, sheriff," he gasped, "there's a black guy wrapped in chains, drowned in the lake!"

"Now ain't that just like a nigger," drawled the sheriff, "to take more chain than he can swim with?"

□   □   □

What has six legs and goes "Ho-de-do, ho-de-do, ho-de-do?"
   Three blacks running for the elevator.

□   □   □

Why do black women have such big purses?
   To carry their lipstick.

□   □   □

Why don't blacks take aspirin?
   They're too proud to pick the cotton out of the bottle.

□   □   □

Little Titus was fooling around on the back porch one day and came across a can of white paint. He proceeded to paint his face and hands with it and run into the kitchen. "Look, Ma, I'm a white boy now!" he shouted.
   "God*DAMN*, Titus, you black as the ace of spades and don't you forget it! Now go wash up before some-one sees you."
   Crestfallen, Titus went in search of his father, say-ing, "Look, Daddy, I'm a white boy now!"
   GodDAMN, boy," roars his father, "you stupid or what? Go wash that crap off before I take my belt to you!"

"You know, Daddy," says Titus, "I've only been white for five minutes or so, and already I'm beginning to hate you niggers."

□   □   □

Why are black men hung better than white men?
Because little white boys had *toys* to play with.

□   □   □

Why don't their mothers let little black kids play in the sandbox?
Because the cats bury them.

Jewish

What's a Jewish dilemma?
Free ham.

□   □   □

At the conclusion of the physical exam the doctor summoned his patient into his office with a very grave look on his face. "I hate to be the one to break it to you, Fred," he said, but I'm afraid you've got cancer. An advanced case, too—you've only got six months to live."

"Oh my God," gasped Fred, turning white. When the news had sunk in he said, "Listen, Doc, you've known me a long time. Do you have any suggestions as to how I could make the most of my remaining months?"

"Have you ever married?" asked the doctor.

Fred explained that he'd been a bachelor all his life.

"You might think about taking a wife," the doctor proposed. "After all you'll need someone to look after you during the final illness."

"That's a good point, Doc," mused Fred. "And

with only six months to live I'd better make the most of my time."

"May I make one more suggestion?" asked the doctor. When Fred nodded, he said, "Marry a Jewish girl."

"A Jewish girl—how come?" wondered Fred.

"It'll seem longer."

□ □ □

Three nice Jewish widows decided to take an exotic vacation together, so off they went to darkest Africa on a photographic safari. The expedition pitched their tents deep in the jungle and the next morning set out on their first excursion, but Naomi was too tired to go along, despite her companions' dismay. And no sooner were they out of earshot than a huge gorilla swept down from a tree, grabbed Naomi, and dragged her off to his nest to screw her mercilessly for three days. On that night, Sophie and Zelda, hysterical with grief, found a battered and bloody Naomi, semiconscious, outside their tent. Naomi was immediately airlifted back to Mount Sinai Hospital in New York where her two friends hovered by her side until, after many days, she was able to speak.

"Naomi, darling, speak to us," beseeched her friends. "Did that creature abuse you? Are you in pain? What's wrong? Say something!"

"What should I say? He never calls," sobbed Naomi, "he never writes . . ."

□ □ □

How do you know when a JAP's having an orgasm?
She drops her emery board.

◻   ◻   ◻

You can imagine the excitement when a Martian space-ship landed in a sunny suburban field and proved to be filled with intelligent, amicable beings. Jane Pauley managed to be the first television personality on the scene, and the chief Martian agreed to an exclusive interview on the "Today" show the next morning. As the cameras started to roll, she told the Martian how curious people on Earth were about his people, so she thought she'd just ask him a few general questions. The Martian graciously said that was fine with him.

"Tell me," said Pauley, nervously clearing her throat, "do all of your people have seven fingers and toes?"

"Yes," said the Martian, waving his slender green appendages in the air.

"And two heads? Everyone has those?"

"Oh yes," said the Martian, nodding both enthusiastically.

"And also those lovely diamonds and rubies embedded in their chests as you do?" asked Pauley.

"Certainly not," snapped the Martian. "Only the Jews."

◻   ◻   ◻

What's the difference between a JAP and poverty?
Poverty sucks.

◻   ◻   ◻

Did you hear about the new Jewish bank?
When you call up, the teller complains, "You never

come by. You never write. You only call when you want money."

□   □   □

Did you hear about the bum who walked up to the Jewish mother on the street and said, "Lady, I haven't eaten in three days."

"Force yourself," she replied.

□   □   □

A young Jewish man takes his mother to a movie about life in ancient Rome. She's from the old country and has a little difficulty following the customs in this strange land, so at one point she asks her son to explain a scene in progress. "This particular scene," he whispers, "shows how in those days the Romans often persecuted the Christians by throwing them in the arena to be devoured by lions."

Studying the gory image for a few moments, she points her finger at a lion in the far corner and shouts, "And dat vun—vy isn't he eating?"

□   □   □

What's a JAP's idea of natural childbirth?
Absolutely no makeup.

□   □   □

Mr. Cohen emigrated to the United States as a young man and fulfilled the immigrant's dream: He ran his own profitable nail factory in Brooklyn, bought a nice house, sent his kids to college, even put the oldest son through Harvard Business School. When the young man graduates, Mr. Cohen says to him, "Moishe, you're a smart one, and I'm going to turn the business over to you and retire to Miami Beach."

A year later he gets an excited call from Moishe. "Dad, things are going great: I've computerized inventory, automated the factory, even got a great new ad campaign. You've gotta come see with your own eyes."

So he picks Mr. Cohen up at the airport, and just before they reach the factory a huge billboard looms up. It's a close-up of Jesus on the cross, with the slogan USE COHEN'S NAILS FOR THE TOUGHEST JOBS. "Oy, Moishe," groans Mr. Cohen, "is that your new campaign? I'm telling you, the goys are never going to go for it."

A year later Moishe calls again. "Dad, you gotta come up again and see how great things are going. And by the way, you were right about that ad campaign; we've got a whole new one now." So Mr. Cohen flies up again and on the way from the airport he sees the same giant billboard. This time it's a picture of Jesus crumpled in a heap at the foot of the cross, and the slogan is YOU SHOULDA USED COHEN'S NAILS.

□   □   □

What's a Jewish porno film?
Ten minutes of sex, fifty minutes of guilt.

□   □   □

How about the new disease affecting Jewish women?
It's called MAIDS—if they don't get one, they die.

What do you get when you cross a JAP and an Apple?
A computer that never goes down.

□   □   □

Why did the Jewish mother have herself entombed at Bloomingdale's?
So her daughter would visit at least twice a week.

□   □   □

The Jewish grandmother was terribly proud of her four-month-old grandson, so she took him with her down to Miami Beach. The first morning she got him all decked out, and down they went to the beach, where she set him by the shore to play. But no sooner had she sat down in her beach chair than a huge tidal wave rose up and swept the baby away.

"God," she said, standing up and shaking her fist at the sky, "you aren't very nice! Here was this little baby boy, whose mother carried him for nine months, barely around for four. We haven't even had time to get to know him or give him a happy life."

In another instant the wave returned, setting the infant down unharmed on the sand. The grandmother looked him over, looked right back at the sky, and snapped, "He had a hat!"

□   □   □

How did they know Jesus was Jewish?
Because he lived at home until he was thirty, he went into his father's business, his mother thought he was God—and he thought his mother was a virgin.

□   □   □

Did you hear about the new movie called *Altered Suits*?
It's the story of a Jewish man who takes acid and buys retail.

□   □   □

What do you get when you cross a JAP and a hooker?
Someone who sucks credit cards.

□   □   □

If Tarzan and Jane were Jewish, what would Cheetah be?
A fur coat.

□   □   □

Mr. Cohn, Mr. Katz, and Mr. Rabinowitz are such avid golfers that their wives finally get fed up with being "golf widows" and insist on a two-week vacation in Miami Beach. On pain of divorce, each promises not to even mention golf to his wife. But by the third day all three are climbing the walls, and sure enough where do they run into each other on the fourth day but the local golf course. "You wouldn't believe this, fellas," moans Cohn, "but this game is costing me, $45,000 for a new Mercedes for my wife."

"You think that's bad," says Katz, "listen to this: I gotta shell out $110,000 for a new condominium."

Rabinowitz smiles and says, "You poor schmucks, I'm here without it costing me a penny. At six A.M. I rolled over and said, 'Well, Becky, what's it going to be, golf course or intercourse?' She says, 'Take a sweater so you shouldn't catch cold.'"

□   □   □

What does the Jewish Santa Claus say as he comes down the chimney?
   "Ho-ho-ho! Anybody want to buy some toys?"

□   □   □

What's the hardest thing for a JAP about having a colostomy?
   Trying to find shoes to match the bag.

Wasp

*H*ow can you tell a male WASP is sexually excited? By the stiff upper lip.

□ □ □

Two WASPs were walking down the street. One turned to the other and said, "You know, you're my best friend but you never ask how I'm doing, how things are going, how's business?"

"Okay," said his friend, "how's business, how are things?"

"Fine."

□ □ □

How does a WASP propose marriage?

He asks, "How would you like to be buried with my people?"

□ □ □

How many WASPs does it take to plan a trip to Israel? Two. One to ask where, and one to ask why.

□   □   □

Why don't they use WASPs to pick cotton?
    They might get lost.

□   □   □

What does a WASP get when her car won't start?
    A very emotionally trying day.

□   □   □

What's the definition of a WASP?
    Someone who gets out of the shower to pee.

□   □   □

How many WASPs does it take to change a lightbulb?
    Answer #1: One.
    Answer #2: Six. One to change the bulb and five to write the environmental impact report.
    Answer #3: Two. One to mix the martinis and one to call the electrician.

□   □   □

How can you tell the bride at a WASP wedding?
    She's the one kissing the golden retriever.

□   □   □

Why did God create WASPs?
    Somebody had to buy retail.

Hear about the disadvantaged WASP?
  He grew up with a black-and-white TV.

□   □   □

What do you get when you cross a Jew and a WASP?
  A pushy Pilgrim.

□   □   □

What do you get when you cross a black and a WASP?
  An abortion.

□   □   □

What's a WASP's idea of open-mindedness?
  Dating a Canadian.

Ethnic Variegated

A Jew and a Chinaman were in a bar together. The Jew brought up the subject of Pearl Harbor, reprimanding the Chinaman for the disgraceful role his countrymen had played. He protested vehemently, pointing out that the raid had been made by the Japanese, and that China was in no way to blame.

"Japanese, Chinese, they're all the same to me," retorted the Jew.

Pretty soon the Chinese fellow started talking about the tragic sinking of the *Titanic*, asking the guy if he didn't feel some degree of personal responsibility about it.

"Hey, wait a minute!" protested the guy. "The Jews didn't have anything to do with the sinking of the *Titanic*—it was sunk by an iceberg!"

"Iceberg, Goldberg," said the Chinaman, "they're all the same to me."

□　□　□

Did you hear about the man who was half Polish and half Italian?

He made himself an offer he couldn't understand.

□   □   □

Mr. Lopez came home unexpectedly and found his wife in bed with another man. Furious, he cried, "What are you doing?"

"See," said Mrs. Lopez, turning to her lover, "I told you he was stupid."

□   □   □

What are the first three words a Puerto Rican child learns?

"Attention K-Mart shoppers . . ."

□   □   □

Why aren't there any Mexican contestants in the summer Olympics?

Because everyone who can run, jump, or swim is already over here.

□   □   □

This big black guy saved all his money for years and years until one day he walked into a Cadillac showroom and put down cash for the car of his dreams, a huge maroon sedan with all the extras. Getting behind the wheel with a huge smile on his face, he called out to the salesman. "Now, tell me, how do I look?"

"Well, you asked for it," said the salesman. "Okay, I see a big buck nigger sitting in a Cadillac, happy as all get-out!"

"*Boy*, I'm glad to hear you say that. I thought you were gonna say, 'There goes another damn Guinea contractor!'"

□   □   □

Paddy O'Casey was on his death bed when his wife Colleen tiptoed into the bedroom and asked if he had any last requests.

"Actually, darlin', there is one thing I really would like before I go off to that great shamrock patch in the sky," Paddy whispered. "A piece of that wonderful chocolate cake of yours."

"Oh, but you can't have that, my dear," his wife exclaimed. "I'm saving it for the wake."

□   □   □

What does an Oriental use for a blindfold?
Dental floss.

□   □   □

A farmer in the Deep South was out looking over his tobacco fields when a bus full of blacks rounded a corner on the country road too fast and rolled over on its side. Losing no time, the farmer ran back to the barn for his pick and shovel, and proceeded to start burying the bus. Just as he was finishing up the job, a state police cruiser arrived on the scene. "Say, didn't a bus fulla black folks just go off the road around here?"

"Yep," replied the farmer.

"Well, where'd they get to?"

"I buried 'em" was the answer.

"Gee," said the trooper, "were they all dead?"

The farmer looked straight at the trooper and said, "Well, some of 'em said they weren't, but you know how they lie."

What do you say to a Puerto Rican in a three-piece suit?
"Will the defendant please rise?"

□   □   □

What do Yoko Ono and the Ethiopians have in common?
Living off dead beetles.

□   □   □

What food do you never see in Ethiopia?
After-dinner mints.

□   □   □

What do you call a seventy-five-pound Ethiopian?
"Fatso."

□   □   □

What's 6-13-6?
The measurements of Miss Ethiopia.

□   □   □

Why is the Ethiopian school day so short?
They skip lunch.

□   □   □

What do you call an Ethiopian in a dinner jacket?
An optimist.

Who's the patron saint of Ethiopia?
Karen Carpenter.

□   □   □

How about the national anthem of Ethiopia?
"Aren't you hungry . . ."

□   □   □

Did you hear about the new Japanese-Jewish restaurant?
It's called So-Sue-Mi.

□   □   □

What do you get when you cross a Jew with a gypsy?
A chain of empty stores.

□   □   □

A Pole was so proud of his new red Cadillac that he just had to show it off, so he cruised through the black part of town. At a stop light, a giant black hauled him out of the driver's seat, drew a circle around him in the road, and told him not to step out of the circle unless he wanted to get the shit beat out of him.

The black guy started to demolish the Caddie, starting with the headlights and windows when he heard the Pole laughing. He moved on to the body and engine, but in between crashes he couldn't help hearing the Pole's hysterical giggles. Finally the black guy came over with his crowbar and said, "What in hell you laughin' at? Your fancy car's never gonna run again."

Snickering, the Pole replied, "So? Ever since

you've been tearing up my car, I've been stepping in and out of this circle."

□   □   □

What do you call a fat Chinaman?
    A chunk.

□   □   □

Unaware of each other's presence, an Arab in his tank and an Israeli in his are motoring up opposite sides of the same hill. The two tanks reach the top of the hill at precisely the same instant, and there is a tremendous crash.
    The Arab soldier climbs hastily through the hatch of his tank, his arms raised in a gesture of surrender.
    Just as quickly, the Israeli leaps from his tank screaming, "WHIPLASH!"

□   □   □

What's the Haitian national anthem?
    "Row, row, row your boat . . ."

□   □   □

An American, a Pole, and an Italian all hear about a legendary bridge: If you have the courage to jump off it, and the presence of mind to shout in midair what you want to become, your wish will be granted. So they make the trek to the bridge and the American says he'll be daring and jump first. Over he goes, yells "Billionaire!" and lands safely on the deck chair of his giant yacht. The Italian jumps next, shouts "An eagle!" and soars up into the heavens. The Pole runs for the edge, stubs his toe on the curb as he jumps, and yells "Oh, shit!"

□   □   □

How about the Japanese factory that spray-painted all their new robots black?

They were two hours late to work the next day.

□   □   □

Why are Mexicans buying up all the Cabbage Patch dolls?

To get birth certificates.

□   □   □

Fabio and Nunzio rent a private plane for the day and are doing fine until it's time for touchdown. Fabio is busy with all the instrument readings and finally gets the plane down, but has to screech to a stop. "Boy, that's a short runway," he says, wiping his forehead.

"Yes," agrees Nunzio, "but look how wide it is."

□   □   □

Why did the Polish couple decide to have only four children?

Because they read in the newspaper that one out of every five babies born in the world today is Chinese.

Did you hear about the psychic Puerto Rican who knew the exact day and minute he would die?

The warden told him.

□   □   □

Have you heard about the Italian girl who flunked her driver's license test?

When the car stalled, from force of habit she jumped into the back seat.

□   □   □

What do you call a Vietnamese family with one dog?
Vegetarians.

□   □   □

What do you call a Vietnamese family with two dogs?
Ranchers.

□   □   □

A Chinaman walked into a bar and said to the black bartender, "I'll have a jigger, nigger."

"You weren't trying to insult me, were you, pal?" asked the bartender. The Chinaman reassured him to the contrary. "Then let's change places," suggested the bartender. They did, and the black walked up the bar and said, "Gimme a drink, chink."

The Chinaman replied, "Sorry, we don't serve niggers."

Two Poles couldn't figure out how to measure a flagpole they'd been hired to paint by the foot, so they asked a black man who was passing by if he would help.

The black pulled a pin from the bottom of the pole, laid the pole on the ground, pulled out his ruler, and measured it. When he was finished, he put his tape measure away, put the flag pole back in its stand, and left.

Once out of earshot, the one Polack turned to the other and said, "Isn't it just like a nigger, you ask for the height and he gives you the width."

□   □   □

Who killed more Indians than Custer?
Union Carbide.

□   □   □

Have you heard the new Union Carbide corporate song?
"One little, two little, three little Indians . . ."

□   □   □

What do you get when you cross and Irishman and a Jew?
An alcoholic who buys his liquor wholesale.

□   □   □

What did the black kid get for Christmas?
My bike.

Did you hear that Alitalia and El Al were merging to form a new airline?

It's going to be called Well I'll Tell Ya . . .

□   □   □

What did the South African girl give her boyfriend?

Apart-head.

□   □   □

What do you get when you cross a Chinaman and a hooker?

Someone who'll suck your laundry.

□   □   □

Three men in an airplane crash died and went to hell. They happened to catch the Devil in a good mood, and he told them that for twenty dollars apiece they could return to earth alive. After the offer was discussed for a bit, the Irishman pulled out $20 and—POOF!—found himself back at home.

"What the hell happened to you?" asked his wife. After he explained, she asked curiously, "So where are the other two?"

"Got me," said the Irishman. "When I left, the Jew had the Devil down to $17.50 and the black said he should be getting a check from the government any day now."

□   □   □

Why's a car engine like an Italian girl?

On a cold morning when you really need it, it won't turn over.

□   □   □

What do you get when you cross a Jew and a Puerto Rican?
A superintendent who thinks he owns the building.

□   □   □

What do you call a Puerto Rican midget?
A speck.

Helen Keller

What's Helen Keller's favorite color?
Corduroy.

□   □   □

How did Helen Keller burn her ear?
Answering the iron.

□   □   □

Did you hear about the Helen Keller doll?
Wind it up and it walks into walls.

□   □   □

How did her parents punish her when she wouldn't do her homework?
They stomped on her Braille books with golf shoes.

What did Helen Keller say as she was making love to her new boyfriend?

"Funny, you don't feel Jewish."

□ □ □

Why does Helen Keller masturbate with one hand?

So she can moan with the other.

□ □ □

Why did Helen Keller marry a black man?

It was easy to read his lips.

Handicapped

*H*ow did the dead baby cross the road?
    Stapled to the chicken.

□   □   □

This beautiful young paraplegic was sitting on the beach in her wheelchair, gazing mournfully out at the crashing waves, when a handsome guy came up behind her. "What's wrong?" he asked gently. "Why do you look so sad?"

"I've never been kissed," she explained, brushing a tear off her cheek.

"Well, I can take care of that," said the fellow, and did, then walked off down the beach feeling pretty pleased with himself.

The next week he was walking down the beach again when what should he see but the same beautiful young paraplegic, looking more down-in-the-mouth than ever. "What's wrong now?" he asked, looking deep into her eyes.

"I've never been fucked," she said sadly.

"No problem," he said, his chest swelling with

manly pride. He bent over to lift her from the wheelchair, cradled her gently in his arms, and walked slowly down the pier. Reaching the end, he threw her in the water and shouted, "Now you're fucked!"

□   □   □

What's the difference between Quasimodo and a messy room?
　　You can straighten up a messy room.

□   □   □

Why did the man like having a midget for a girlfriend?
　　Because she always wanted to go up on him.

□   □   □

What do you do when an epileptic has a fit in your bathtub?
　　Throw in your laundry.

□   □   □

This guy has a blind date, and when she comes to the door his worst fears are realized: she's a paraplegic. But he takes her out to dinner and the movies anyway, being a nice guy, and in the movie theater it doesn't take long for things to work up to the heavy-breathing stage. Still, there she is in her wheelchair, and he's pretty perplexed about how to take things to the next stage . . . if there's going to be a next stage.
　　"Don't worry," she whispers in his ear. "Take me to the playground, and I'll hang from the jungle gym."
　　So he does just that, and they manage to have a

pretty good time. She gets a little dirty and scratched up in the process though, and he's somewhat apprehensive when her father comes to the door to let her in.

"You see, sir . . ." he begins, but her father interrupts him with effusive thanks. "Don't worry about a thing, young man. The last three guys left her hanging there."

□ □ □

What's black and blue and goes tha-dump, tha-dump?
A baby in a dryer.

□ □ □

What's the hardest thing about eating vegetables?
The wheelchairs.

□ □ □

The bus driver was training a new kid to take over his route. At one stop a middle-aged woman was waiting, and when the driver waved to her, she waved back. She held up her index finger, at which the driver shook his head and held up his index and middle finger. She pointed her thumb up and the driver shook his head vigorously and pointed his thumb down. To the new kid's astonishment, the woman then started fondling her tits, to which the driver responded by scratching his balls. And the woman gave him the finger and walked off.

"What the hell was that all about?" asked the kid. "Was she crazy or something?"

"Nah," said the driver, "just deaf. See, she asked me if this was Bus #1 and I told her it was #2. She asked if we were going uptown and I said no, down-town. Then she wanted to know if we were going to the Dairy Queen and I said no, to the ball park. So she said, 'Fuck you, I'll walk.'"

□   □   □

I'll say one thing about polio—
    It keeps the kids off the streets.

□   □   □

What does it take to make a dead baby float?
    One scoop of ice cream and a scoop of dead baby.

□   □   □

The anatomy lesson for the week was the way in which the body of a handicapped person compensates for its deficiencies. As an example the professor showed a slide of a man with no legs whose arms and shoulders had consequently become hugely muscled. "Your assign-ment," he instructed a pretty medical student, "is to find someone who has compensated for a physical hand-icap and to report on it for the class."

    After class the student went into the bar next door, and what should she catch sight of but a hunchback nursing a beer at the bar. Screwing up her courage, she went over and told him about her assignment. "If you don't mind my asking," she said sweetly, "is there some part of your anatomy which has compensated for your handicap?"

    "As a matter of fact there is," said the hunchback. "Come up to my place and I'll show you." When they got upstairs, he dropped his pants and revealed the big-gest cock she had ever seen. Kneeling down, she couldn't resist touching it, then caressing it, then rubbing it against her face.

"Jesus Christ, don't blow it!" screamed the hunchback, jumping back. "That's how I got the hump on my back."

□   □   □

What's the height of cheapness?
    Taking an anorexic to dinner.

□   □   □

What's the perfect gift for a dead baby?
    A dead puppy.

□   □   □

What do elephants use for vibrators?
    Epileptics.

□   □   □

The Joneses were understandably disturbed when their first child was born with no ears, and their best friends, the Smiths, were well aware of this. Preparing for their first visit to view the newborn, Mrs. Smith reminded her husbands to avoid at all costs any references to the baby's defect.

A little while later the Smiths found themselves cooing over the crib with the new parents. "Look at those long fingers," said Mrs. Smith admiringly. "Why, I bet he'll be a pianist. Or an athlete—look at those big, strong legs. And those huge blue eyes . . . how's his vision?"

"Terrific," said the proud mother.

"It'd better be," blurted Smith, "cause he'll never be able to wear glasses!"

□ □ □

Why can't midgets use tampax?
They trip over the strings.

□ □ □

What's small, screams, and can't turn corners?
A baby with a spear through it.

□ □ □

A man with a bad stuttering problem had never married, but one day he met the woman of his dreams, a lovely young epileptic. After a whirlwind courtship the two were married, and after the ceremony they headed for a honeymoon hotel in the Poconos. Five minutes after they'd registered, the phone rang at the front desk.

"Cccome qqquick and bbbring a rrrope," the man yelled into the manager's ear.

After a desperate search for a rope, the manager raced up the stairs. There on the bed, naked, was the wife in the midst of a seizure. The husband grabbed the rope from the manager, proceeded to tie her to the bed and then climbed up on top of her.

"Okay," he shouted, "cccut hhher lllloose!"

Leper

What's the advantage of being visited by a leper prostitute?

    She leaves so much behind for you to remember her by.

      □   □   □

Why was the leper so embarrassed?

    He stuck his foot in his mouth.

      □   □   □

Why did the leper flunk his driver's test?

    He left his foot on the gas.

      □   □   □

What's small, green, and falls apart?

    A leperchaun.

Why did the leper go to the political rally?
Because he wanted to give somebody a piece of his mind.

□   □   □

Why didn't the leper cross the road?
He lost his nerves.

□   □   □

How come the leper couldn't speak?
The cat got his tongue.

□   □   □

Hear about the new Scratch 'n Sniff stickers for lepers?
They include a nose.

□   □   □

What do you get when you screw a leper?
A piece of ass.

□   □   □

What did the leper say to the prostitute?
Keep the tip.

□   □   □

What do you call a leper with herpes?
Redundant.

What do you call a leper with herpes who also has AIDS?
Trendy.

Celebrities

*D*id you hear about the all-expenses-paid vacation for losers?

—Grace Kelly drives you to the airport.

—Thurman Munson flies you to a remote tropical island.

—Ted Kennedy's your chauffeur on the island.

—You go yachting with Natalie Wood.

—You have drinks with William Holden.

—And Roman Polanski stays home and watches your kids.

□ □ □

What's the difference between Willie Nelson and Dean Martin?

Willie Nelson is an older country Western singer, and Dean Martin is a singer older than most Western countries.

□ □ □

If Castro were gay, what would you call his lover?

An infidel.

□   □   □

Did you see the new movie out starring O. J. Simpson and Barbra Streisand?

It's called *Rentl*.

□   □   □

Know why the National Hockey League drafted Indira Gandhi?

She stopped seven shots in four seconds.

□   □   □

How can you tell Dolly Parton's kids in the playground?

Stretch marks on their lips.

□   □   □

What did the doctor tell Rock Hudson when he contracted AIDS?

"Don't worry, you'll be back on your knees in no time."

□   □   □

What was Karen Carpenter's favorite saying?

"Gag me with a spoon."

□   □   □

You heard about Michael Jackson and Richard Pryor's new charity?

The Ignited Negro College Fund.

What's the Fund's motto?
"The mind is a terrible thing to baste."

□   □   □

Hear about the movie starring Sylvester Stallone and Rock Hudson?
It's called "Rambutt."

□   □   □

What do Alex Haley and Suzanne Somers have in common?
Black roots.

□   □   □

Did you hear they're building an archive for the Nixon papers?
No admission charge—but you have to break in.

□   □   □

What's yellow and sleeps alone?
Yoko Ono.

□   □   □

Did you hear about Evel Knievel's latest stunt?
He's going to run across Ethiopia with a sandwich tied to his back.

□   □   □

What was the most erotic thing ever said on TV?
"Gee, Ward, you were kind of rough on the Beaver last night."

□   □   □

Why did Karen Carpenter shoot her dog?
  It kept trying to bury her.

□   □   □

Why are they going to put Rock Hudson in his casket face down?
  So all his friends can recognize him!

□   □   □

Why didn't Natalie Wood shower on the boat?
  She preferred to wash up on shore.

□   □   □

What did Grace Kelly have that Natalie Wood could've used?
  A good stroke.

□   □   □

Do you know why Hitler committed suicide?
  He got the gas bill.

□   □   □

Why can't you go to the bathroom at the Beatles concert?
  There's no John.

What were the last words Marvin Gaye's father said to him?

"This is the last 45 you'll ever hear."

□   □   □

How did Marvin Gaye die?

He heard it through the carbine.

□   □   □

Why didn't Karen Carpenter visit pool halls a lot?

She didn't like it when people chalked her head.

Male Anatomy

What was the first thing Adam said to Eve?
"Stand back! I don't know how big this thing gets!"

□　□　□

One day Bobby's teacher tells the class they're going to play a thinking game, and asks for a volunteer. "Pick me, pick me," begs Bobby.

"Okay, Bobby," says the teacher. "Now I'm going to describe objects to you and you tell me what they are. Here we go: what's red, shiny, and you eat it?"

"A cherry," says Bobby.

"No, it's an apple, but it shows you're thinking," said the teacher gently. "Ready for the next one? What's yellow and you eat it?"

"A lemon," says Bobby.

"No," says the teacher, "it's a banana, but it shows you're thinking."

Before the teacher can continue, Bobby interrupts. "Okay, teacher, I've got one for you." He reaches into his pocket, looks down, pulls his hand out, and asks, "What's long, pink, and has a little red head on the end of it?"

"Ooh, Bobby!" squeals the teacher.
"No, it's a match—but it shows you're thinking."

□   □   □

Why did God create men?
Because you can't teach an electric vibrator to mow the lawn.

□   □   □

One day a young woman was walking home when a man grabbed her, dragged her into a back alley, and started molesting her. "Help! Help me, someone," she cried. "I'm being robbed!"

"You ain't being robbed, lady," interrupted the man, "you're being screwed."

"Well if this is being screwed," she said, "I'm being robbed."

□   □   □

A urologist claimed that he could find any disease just by testing a person's urine. One man, who had tennis elbow, decided to fool the doctor. He made an appointment, received his specimen bottle, and was told to come back the next day. That night he urinated in the bottle, then his wife did, followed by his daughter, and then the family dog. Then he beat off in it. He returned the next day with his sample and gave it to the doctor for testing. Four hours went by before the doctor came out. He was just sweating bullets. "You know," he said, "it took me a long time, but I think I've finally got it. Your wife has V.D., your daughter is pregnant, your dog has mange, and if you'd quit beating off, you wouldn't have tennis elbow."

□   □   □

A horny young woman had exhausted the sexual capacities of all her male acquaintances, so she decided to put an ad in the local paper. The ad was quite explicit about the nature of the services in which she was interested and received quite an enthusiastic response, and the young woman made dates with a number of the more likely-sounding candidates. But none of the men came up to her rather demanding standards, and the final disillusionment came one night when she opened the door to a man with no arms and no legs on her doormat.

After listening to his explanation that he was responding to the ad in the paper, the young woman broke in. "Listen, pal," she said, "I don't mean to be rude or crude, but I'm not interested in polite conversation, if you catch my drift, and you don't exactly look like great Romeo material . . ."

"Hey, lady," interrupted the man, "I rang the doorbell, didn't I?"

□   □   □

There was this guy who desperately wanted to have sex with his girlfriend. However, he was too embarrassed because of his extremely small penis. So one night, he took her to a dark place where she couldn't see it and, after furiously making out with her, dropped his pants and put his penis in her hand.

"Sorry, I don't smoke," she whispered.

□   □   □

What's the difference between light and hard?
1) It's light all day.
2) You can sleep with a light on.

□   □   □

One day a mouse was driving along the road in his Mercedes when he heard an anguished roaring noise coming from the side of the road. Stopping the car, he got out and discovered a lion stuck in a deep ditch and roaring for help. Reassuring the lion, the mouse tied a rope around the axle of the Mercedes, threw the other end down to the lion, and pulled the beast out of the ditch. The lion thanked the mouse profusely and they went their separate ways.

Two weeks later the lion was out for a stroll in the country when he heard a panicked squeaking coming from the side of the road. Investigating the noise, what should he come across but the mouse stuck in the same hole. "Oh, please help me, Mr. Lion," squeaked the terrified mouse. "I saved you with my car once, remember?"

"Course I'll help you, little feller," roared the lion. "I'll just lower my dick down to you, you hold on to it, and we'll have you out of there in a jiffy." Sure enough, a few minutes later the mouse was high and dry on the roadside, trying to convey his eternal gratitude to the lion.

"Don't give it another thought," said the lion kindly. "It just goes to show that if you've got a big dick, you don't need a Mercedes."

□   □   □

One day Little Herbie heard a noise from his parents' room and opened the door to see them screwing. "What're you doing, Dad?" he asked.

"Just playing gin rummy with your mother," was the answer.

On the way back downstairs, Little Herbie heard a noise coming from his grandparents' room, opened the door, and asked what was going on. His granddad explained he was just playing gin rummy with his grandmother.

Not too much later, dinner was served and everyone came to the table but Little Herbie. Looking in his room, Herbie's father found him lying on his bed, the sheets flapping up and down. "I'm just playing gin rummy," explained the boy.

"But you've got no one to play with," said his dad sternly.

"That's okay, Dad; with a hand like this, you don't need a partner."

□   □   □

Why did God make man first?
  He didn't want a woman looking over his shoulder.

□   □   □

A man is strolling on the beach when he comes across a lamp lying in the sand. He rubs it and, sure enough, a genie pops out. "I will grant you your one true desire," booms the huge, turbaned figure.

"Wow, that's really great!" exclaims the man. "I wish my dick touched the ground."

So the genie cut his legs off.

□   □   □

Explaining to his doctor that his sex life wasn't all it could be, Milt asked his doctor for a pill that would enable him to get it up for his wife. It so happened that the doctor had just the right medication, so Milt took a pill and drove home. But when he got to the apartment his wife wasn't at home, and after waiting for an hour or so in growing discomfort, Milt finally had to jerk off.

When the doctor called to check in the next day, Milt explained what had happened. "Well, gee, Milt, you didn't have to do for yourself," pointed out the doctor. "There are other women in the building."

"Doctor," said Milt, "for other women I don't need a pill."

□　□　□

What can Lifesavers do that a man can't?
　　Come in five different flavors.

□　□　□

One night after their proprietor was asleep, the parts of the body were arguing about which had the toughest job. "I've really got it rough," bemoaned the feet. "He puts me in these smelly sneakers, makes me jog till I've got blisters . . . it's brutal!"

"You got nothing to complain about," maintained the stomach. "Last night I got nothing but bourbon, pizza, and aspirin. It's a miracle I kept it together."

"Oh quit bitching, you two," moaned the penis. "Every night, I'm telling you, he sticks me in a dark tunnel and makes me do push-ups until I throw up."

□　□　□

What's twelve inches long and white?
　　Nothing.

□   □   □

Three guys were walking down the street when they were suddenly stopped by a big black guy who jumps out in front of them. "You better have ten inches of dick between the three of you, or I might have to have some fun with my knife," he says, pulling out a switchblade.

The first guy cooly whips out his five-incher. The second guy isn't far behind with his four-incher, and the third produces his one-incher. Satisfied, the black guy lets them go.

The three head off around the corner, where the first guy gasps, "Good thing I had my five-incher."

The second guy says, "Yeah, and we're lucky I had my four inches."

"No kidding," says the third guy. "Thank God I had a hard-on!"

□   □   □

This fellow married a virgin and wanted to go to special pains to make sure her sexual inexperience wasn't to be a cause of any tension or trouble. He explained that he didn't want her ever to feel pressured into having sex with him, but wanted it to come of her own free will.

"In fact, darling," he said to her tenderly, "I think we should set up a secret system to make all this as clear and simple as possible. Here's how it'll work: when you want to have sex, pull my penis once; when you don't want to, pull my penis a hundred times."

□   □   □

A married woman is entertaining her lover one rainy afternoon when her husband unexpectedly comes home early from work. "Quick, out on the roof," hisses the woman, pushing him out the bedroom window and closing it just as her husband's footsteps reach the top of the stairs.

Crouched on the roof in the rain, the boyfriend is naked except for a rubber and is wondering what the hell his next move should be. The first person in sight is a jogger and the boyfriend takes a deep breath, jumps off the roof, and falls into step alongside the jogger as nonchalantly as possible. After a block and a half the jogger can no longer contain his curiosity and asks, "Say, you always wear that thing when you run?"

"Naw," says the boyfriend coolly, "only when it rains."

□ □ □

What's the difference between meat and fish?
    If you beat your fish, it dies.

□ □ □

What's the definition of macho?
    Jogging home from your own vasectomy.

□ □ □

A little embarrassed, the patient cleared his throat before explaining his rather unusual problem. "YOU SEE, DOC," he boomed in a voice so deep and raspy it was almost impossible to understand, "I CAN'T GO ON WITH THIS VOICE ANY MORE—IT'S DRIVING ME CRAZY. CAN YOU FIX IT SO I SOUND LIKE A NORMAL PERSON?"

"I'll certainly try," said the doctor. After examining the patient, he reported that some sort of weight was pulling on the vocal cords and distorting the voice. "Any idea what it could be?" he queried.

The patient cleared his throat again. "ACTUALLY DOC, I HAPPEN TO BE . . . UH . . . ESPE-CIALLY WELL ENDOWED, AND MAYBE THAT'S WHAT'S DOING IT. LISTEN, IF YOU HAVE TO REMOVE SOME OF IT, THAT'S FINE BY ME. I'LL DO *ANYTHING* TO GET A VOICE LIKE A REGULAR GUY." So the doctor went ahead and performed the operation.

Two weeks later the patient telephoned the doctor's office. "Hey doc," he babbled happily, "I can't thank you enough. Finally I sound like anyone else—it's just great! After a pause, he asked, "Say, by the way, what'd you do with the piece of my penis you removed?"

"I THREW IT AWAY," said the doctor.

□ □ □

What did the elephant say to the naked man?
"How d'you breathe through that thing?"

Female Anatomy

What do you call a woman who can suck a golf ball through fifty feet of garden hose?

Darling.

□ □ □

God has just spent six days creating the heavens and the earth, and since it's the seventh day of rest, He and Gabriel are sitting back and admiring His handiwork.

"You know, God," says Gabriel, "you have done one hell of a job—excuse my language. Those snowy peaks are unbelievable majestic, and the woods, with those little sunny dells and meadows . . . masterful. Not to mention the oceans: those fantastic coral reefs and all the sea creatures and the waves crashing on the beaches. And all the animals—from fleas to elephants— what a job. Not to mention the heavens; how could I leave them out? What a touch, that Milky Way."

God beams.

"I just have the smallest suggestion, if you'll excuse my presumption," says Gabriel. "You know those sample humans you put down there in the Garden of Eden?"

God nods, a frown furrowing His brow.

"Well," says Gabriel, "I was just wondering whether, for all the obvious reasons, they shouldn't have differing sets of genitalia as all the other animals do?"

God reflects on this for a minute, and then a smile crosses His face. "You're right," He exclaims. "Give the dumb one a cunt!"

□   □   □

What are the three best things about being a woman?

You can bleed without cutting yourself;

You can bury a bone without digging a hole;

And you can make a man come without calling him.

□   □   □

As the newlywed couple was checking into the hotel for their honeymoon, another couple at the desk offered to show them around the town that night. Thanking them for the kind offer, the bridegroom explained that it was their wedding night and that they'd prefer to take a rain check.

When the second couple came down to breakfast the next morning they were astonished to catch sight of the groom in the hotel bar apparently drowning his sorrows. "Why, you should be the happiest man in the world today," they said, coming over to him.

"Yesterday I was," said the man mournfully, "but this morning, without realizing it, I put three ten-dollar bills on the pillow and got up to get dressed."

"Hey, cheer up, she probably didn't even notice."

"That's the problem," the groom went on. "Without even thinking, she gave me five dollars change."

□   □   □

What do you call a truckload of vibrators?
  Toys for twats.

□   □   □

A certain virginal and shy college freshman was lucky to have a roommate who was considerably more experienced. When the bashful boy broke down and explained his predicament, his roommate was quick to offer to set him up with the campus floozie. "Just take her out to dinner and show and then let nature take its course," he explained reassuringly. "This girl knows what the score is."

The roommate arranged the date as promised, and the freshman took the coed out for a delightful evening of dining and dancing. On the way home he parked his car in a dark lane, broke out in a cold sweat, and blurted out, "Gosh, I sure would love to have a little pussy."

"I would, too," she sighed. "Mine's the size of a milk pail."

□   □   □

One night little Johnny walked in on his parents while they were screwing. "Daddy," he cried, "what are you and Mommy doing?"

"Uh . . . we're making a little sister for you to play with," stammered his father.

"Oh, neat," said Johnny, and went back to bed.

The next day his dad came home to find the little boy sobbing his eyes out on the front porch. "What's wrong, Johnny?" he asked, picking him up.

"You know the little sister you and Mommy made me?"

"Yes," said his father, blushing.

The little boy wailed, "Today the milkman ate it."

□   □   □

What's the best thing about Women's Liberation?

It gives you girls something to do in your spare time!

□   □   □

A gigolo marries an ugly, not too bright woman who happens to have loads of money.

One day the man goes out to repair a hole in the roof of the stable. "I'll need a ladder," he says to his wife.

"Get the ladder, get the ladder," she repeats dutifully as she trots off.

"I'll need a hammer and nails," he tells her a bit later.

"Get the hammer, get the nails, get the hammer . . ." as she runs back to the tool shed.

The guy gets down to work and is hammering away when he hits himself squarely on the thumb. "*Fuck!*" he screams.

His wife bobs away, saying, "Get the bag, get the bag!"

□   □   □

What do you call a hooker with no legs?

A nightcrawler.

Mrs. Jones was quite startled when her six-year-old son barged into the bathroom just as she was stepping out of the shower. She hastily covered up, but not before the little boy pointed right at her crotch and asked, "What's that?"

"Oh," she said, thinking fast, "that's where I got hit with an axe."

"Got you right in the cunt, didn't it?"

□　□　□

For months the loving newlywed had asked his bride to give him oral sex, but to no avail. His sweet entreaties never worked, for the blushing bride was simply too innocent and inexperienced to even *think* of such a thing, let alone attempt it. But a year of gentle prersistence finally paid off, and one night his darling nervously but lovingly performed the act. When it was over, she looked deeply into his eyes and asked, "How was I, sweetheart?"

He looked back at her and said, "How should I know—I'm no cocksucker!"

□　□　□

What's 10, 9, 8, 7, 6, 5, 4, 3, 2, 1?
　　Bo Derek getting older.

□　□　□

Why do women have legs?
　　So they don't leave tracks like snails.

What are three things a woman can do that a man can't?
(1) Have a baby.
(2) Have her period.
(3) Get laid when she's dead.

□　□　□

A nymphomaniac goes to the supermarket and gets all hot and bothered eyeing the carrots and cucumbers. By the time she gets to the checkout line she can't hold out much longer, so she asks one of the supermarket baggers to carry her groceries out to the car for her. They're halfway across the lot when the nympho slips her hand down his pants and whispers, "You know, I've got an itchy pussy."

"Sorry, lady," says the bagger, "but I can't tell one of those Japanese cars from another."

□　□　□

What's a perfect 10?
A woman about waist-high with no teeth and a flat head you can rest your drink on.

□　□　□

What's a Cinderella 10?
A woman who sucks and fucks till midnight and then turns into a pizza and a six-pack.

□　□　□

The gynecologist stuck up his head after completing his examination. "I'm sorry, Miss," he said, "but removing that vibrator is going to involve a very lengthy and delicate operation."

"I'm not sure I can afford it," sighed the young woman on the examining table. "Why don't you just replace the batteries?"

□ □ □

This woman goes to the gynecologist for the first time and is rather embarrassed as she puts her feet in the stirrups. The doctor goes around for a look and says, "Why, that's the biggest pussy I've ever seen—the biggest pussy I've ever seen!"

"You didn't have to say it twice," snaps the woman.

"I didn't," says the doctor.

□ □ □

Why did God create women?
Because sheep can't cook.

□ □ □

A mother and a daughter lived together in devastating poverty, so it was cause for great rejoicing when, on her way home from school, the daughter found fifty cents on the sidewalk. She ran home and showed it to her mother, who decided that for fifty cents they could get two eggs and a bottle of ketchup and have a real meal. So off went the daughter to the store.

As luck would have it, the daughter was happily skipping home with the eggs and ketchup when a truck backfired, startling her so much that she dropped the groceries. Staring down at the ruined feast, which was smashed at her feet, she sat down and started to cry.

A man came up behind her and surveyed the scene for a few moments. "There there, honey, don't cry," he said consolingly, "It would have died anyway: its eyes were too far apart."

□   □   □

Where do women airline pilots sit?

In the cuntpit.

□   □   □

The manager of a prosperous whorehouse in Warsaw one night found, to his dismay, that he was short of girls for the evening's entertainment. Thinking quickly, he dashed out and bought several inflatable fuck dolls, figuring that, given his average clientele, no one would know the difference. Soon he ushered a customer into a room that housed one of the new lovelies, assuring him he was in for an especially good time.

When the customer came out of the room a little while later, the manager was waiting eagerly in the hallway. He winked at the fellow and asked, "Well? How'd you like her?"

"I don't know what happened," said the customer, shaking his head. "I bit her on the tit, she farted, and flew out the window."

□   □   □

Why did the woman with the huge pussy douche with Crest?

She heard it reduces cavities.

Why do women have two holes?

So that when they're drunk, you can carry them like a six-pack.

□ □ □

After going through Lamaze, Leboyer, and La Leche classes with his expectant wife, the proud new father remained by his wife's bedside throughout labor and birth, bonding with the newborn child. Wanting to be as sympathetic as possible, he took his wife's hand and said emotionally, "Tell me how it was, darling, tell me how it actually felt to give birth."

His wife replied, "Sure. Smile as hard as you can."

Beaming down beatifically at his wife and child, the father said, "That's not too hard."

She continued, "Now insert your index fingers into the corners of your mouth." He obeyed, still smiling broadly.

"Now stretch your lips as far as it will go. . . ."

"Still not too tough," he commented.

"Right," she retorted. "Now pull them over your head."

□ □ □

Why is a clitoris like Antarctica?

Most men know it's there, but few really care.

□ □ □

Why don't they let women swim in the ocean any more?

They can't get the smell out of the fish.

Once upon a time there was a little girl named Little Red Riding Hood. One fine morning she set out for Grandma's house in her new bonnet and with a freshly baked cake in her basket. But what should she find when she got to grandmas' but a big bad wolf hiding out in Grandma's bed. The wolf jumped up, grabbed Little Red Riding Hood, and snarled, "You've had it, little girl. I'm going to eat you right up."

"Eat, eat, eat," cried Little Red Riding Hood, tearing off her bonnet. "Doesn't anyone *fuck* anymore?"

□   □   □

What's the difference between garbage and a girl from New Jersey?

Sometimes garbage gets picked up.

□   □   □

This guy and girl are making out in the back seat of the car, and things are getting pretty hot and heavy. "Put your finger inside me," she asks, and he's only too happy to oblige.

"Put another finger inside me," she orders, moaning in pleasure.

"Put your whole hand inside me."

"Put both hands inside me."

"Now clap."

"I can't!" the guy protests.

"Tight, huh?" she smiles.

□   □   □

How can you tell if your girlfriend's too fat?

If she sits on your face and you can't hear the stereo.

□ □ □

A guy went to the whorehouse and the madam asked him what sort of activities he preferred. "I have a certain, uh, idiosyncrasy," he admitted.

"Our girls are used to anything." said the madam reassuringly. "Betty, take this gentleman upstairs." Five minutes later there's a piercing scream and Betty comes running down the stairs, followed soon after by the dejected man. The madam insists on knowing just what it is his tastes run to, and finally the guy confesses, "I like to have the broad lay on the floor while I shit on her stomach." The madam says, "Why didn't you say so? Alice is the girl for you." So he goes upstairs with Alice, everything goes according to plan, and the guy enjoys himself so much that he goes back the next night to see Alice and becomes a regular customer, stopping by three or four times a week.

One night he's horny but terrifically constipated, and he goes over to the whorehouse for Alice. They go upstairs and he squats on top of her. But despite massive straining and groaning, he can only manage a tiny fart. At which Alice breaks into heartbreaking sobs. "What's the matter?" he asks, turning around.

Tears running down her cheeks, she weeps, "You don't love me anymore."

□ □ □

How do you fuck a fat girl?
Roll her in flour and go for the wet spot.

□ □ □

It seems there was this woman who hated wearing underwear. One day she decided to go shopping for a new pair of shoes, and since she was wearing a skirt the salesman was enjoying an excellent view. After the third or fourth pair of shoes, the guy couldn't stand it any more. "Lady," he said, "that's some beautiful sight. I could eat that pussy full of ice cream."

Disgusted, the woman ran out of the store and went home. When her husband got home from work she told him about the incident and asked him to go beat the shit out of the salesman. And when he flatly refused, she wanted to know why.

"Three reasons," said her husband. "Number one: you shouldn't have been out in a skirt with no underpants. Number two: you have enough shoes to last you ten more years. And number three: any motherfucker who can eat that much ice cream I don't want to mess with in the first place."

□   □   □

What's the perfect woman?

A deaf, dumb, and blind nymphomaniac who owns a liquor store.

□   □   □

A young man was raised in the Australian outback by his father alone, who, not wanting him to get into any trouble, told him to stay away from women. "They have teeth down there," he explained, and let the impressionable boy's imagination do the rest.

In time, however, the fellow's father died. He saw friends getting married and starting families, and he decided it was time to get on with it. So he found himself a willing girl—who was rather disappointed when the consummation consisted of a peck on the cheek alone. The second night she dolled herself up in her sheerest negligée, only to find that once again he pecked her on the cheek, rolled over, and went to sleep. On the third night she caught him before the snores began and proceeded to give him a brief lecture on the birds and the bees and his conjugal duties.

"Oh, no, you don't!" the new husband cried. "I know about you women. You've got teeth down there, and I ain't coming anywhere near."

Well, the bride roared with laughter and invited her husband around the bed for a close inspection. Cautiously he came over and proceeded to look things over with great care. Finally he stuck up his head.

"You're right," he proclaimed. "You've got no teeth, and your gums are in terrible condition!"

□　□　□

Do you know why women have cunts?
　　So men will talk to them.

Homosexual

Why did the pervert cross the road?
Because his dick was stuck in the chicken.

□   □   □

A gay goes to the proctologist for a routine examination. When the doctor gets him into position, he's quite surprised to find a piece of string dangling from the man's ass. He pulls gently on the string and out pops a lovely bouquet of flowers.

"Do you know I just pulled a dozen roses out of your rectum?" asks the astonished doctor.

"Is that so?" says the patient. "Who're they from?"

□   □   □

What do you call a gay midget?
A low blow.

□   □   □

Why is AIDS a miracle?
"It's the only thing in the world that can change a fruit into a vegetable.

□ □ □

One night Fred came home from work and told his wife over dinner that he had just signed up with the company hockey team. Worried that he might hurt himself, his wife went out the next day to buy him a jockstrap.

The effeminate sales clerk was only too happy to help her.

"They come in colors, you know," he told her. "We have Virginal White, Ravishing Red, and Promiscuous Purple."

"I guess white will do just fine," she said.

"They come in different sizes, too, you know," said the clerk.

"Gee, I'm really not sure what Fred's size is," confessed his wife. So the clerk extended his pinkie.

"No, it's bigger than that."

The clerk extended a second finger.

"No, it's bigger than that," said the wife.

A third finger.

"Still bigger," she said.

When the clerk stuck out his thumb, too, she said, "Yes, that's about right."

So the clerk put all five fingers in his mouth, pulled them out, and announced expertly, "That's a medium."

□ □ □

What does *AIDS* stand for?
Adiós, Infected Dick Sucker.

□ □ □

What do you call a Jewish homosexual?
He-blew.

□   □   □

What do you call an Irish homosexual?
Gay-lick.

□   □   □

What do you call a Chinese homosexual?
Chew-man-chew.

□   □   □

What do you call an Italian homosexual?
A Guinea cocksucker.

□   □   □

Three gays were discussing what they thought their favorite sport would be. The first decides on football, 'cause of all those gorgeous guys bending over in their tight pants.

"Definitely wrestling," sighs the second guy. "Those skimpy little costumes, and think of the holds."

"Definitely baseball," says the third guy. "Why? Well, I'd be pitching with the bases loaded, the batter would hit a line drive right to me, I'd catch it, and I'd just stand there while the other guys rounded the bases. Meanwhile the crowd would be going crazy, screaming, "Throw the ball, you cocksucker!" and that's what I like—recognition."

□   □   □

"My dildo can do anything a man can do." boasted a dyke in a bar one night.

"Oh, yeah?" replied a nearby drunk. "Let's see your dildo get up and order a round of drinks."

□ □ □

What do you get when you cross a gay Eskimo and a black?

A snowblower that doesn't work.

□ □ □

Two gays were having a drink at the bar when an attractive woman walked by. "Mmmmmm . . ." said one appreciatively, eyeing her up and down.

"Oh, Tom!" shrieked his horrified friend. "Don't tell me you're going straight!"

"Nothing like that," said Tom musingly. "It's just that sometimes I can't help wishing I'd been born a lesbian . . ."

□ □ □

Why was the homosexual fired from his job at the sperm bank?

For drinking on the job.

□ □ □

Farmer Jones died during the winter, and when it came time for spring planting, Widow Jones realized she couldn't do all the work herself. So she applied to the town council, only to be told that all the able-bodied farmhands had already been hired and the only two left were an ex-con and a queer. Widow Jones chose the queer, and was pleased to find him a steady and reliable worker. When six weeks of hard labor had gone by, the man asked Widow Jones if he could have Saturday night off to go into town. "All right," she consented, "but be back by nine o'clock."

The farmhand wasn't back until ten-thirty, and as he tiptoed up the stairs he heard Widow Jones summon him to her room. "Take off my shoes," she commanded. He obeyed. "Take off my dress." He did so." "Take off my slip . . . and my stockings . . . and my garter belt."

The queer obeyed without saying a word.

"Now take off my bra," snapped Widow Jones, "and don't you ever borrow my clothes again!"

□   □   □

How do you identify a bull-dyke?

She kick-starts her vibrator and rolls her own tampons.

□   □   □

What kind of soup do they serve in a gay Chinese restaurant?

Cream of Some Young Guy.

□   □   □

What do you get when you cross a black with a homosexual?

An AIDS victim with sickle-cell anemia.

□   □   □

There are these two gay guys who decide they want to have a baby. So they find an obliging lesbian, have her impregnated by sperm donation, and are simply thrilled when she gives birth to a seven-pound baby boy. They rush to the hospital for the first viewing of their son, standing with their noses pressed against the glass of the nursery window and surveying row upon row of squalling infants. Except for one quiet, clean little baby, cooing softly to itself amid all the chaos.

Sure enough, when the gays ask to see their son, the nurse heads for the quiet baby and brings him over for the proud parents to ogle.

"Gee," said one of them to the nurse, "he sure is well behaved compared to the rest of those howling brats, isn't he?"

"Oh, he's quiet now," said the nurse, "but he squalls like all the rest when I take the pacifier out of his ass."

□   □   □

Why can't the scientists figure out what causes AIDS?

They can't train the lab rats to have anal sex.

□   □   □

These two gays wake up one morning and one of them says to the other, "This is terrible. One of us is simply going to have to get a job." The other one says, "You're right. I'll go." So he gets out of bed, takes a shower, and puts on a jacket and tie, but when he walks into the kitchen he sees his lover jerking off into a plastic bag.

"What are you doing *that* for?" he asks.

"Well," says the first gay, "I didn't think you'd be coming home for lunch so I thought I'd pack you one."

"In the center ring," cries the ringmaster, "we have Nero, the boldest and bravest animal trainer in the world. Watch, ladies and gentlemen, as he puts his head between the jaws of our man-eating lion!" The crowd roars as Nero pulls out his head unscathed.

"Now, folks, watch this!" shouts the announcer, as Nero unzips his pants and puts his prick between the giant teeth. "Don't do it!" shrieks the audience as the lion's jaws clamp shut. But without flinching, Nero pulls them open and removed his unharmed penis, and wild cheers fill the arena.

When the noise dies down the ringmaster steps forward and announces, "Ladies and gentlemen, a prize of five thousand, yes, five thousand dollars, to the man in our audience who'll try that trick." His jaw drops as a small, effeminate man steps right up to the ringside. "You're going to repeat that trick with our man-eating lion in front of all these people?" he asks incredulously.

"Certainly," says the fag, "but I must tell you something first. I don't think I can open my mouth as wide was the lion did."

□　□　□

How do you fit four gays at a crowded bar?
　Turn the stool upside down.

□　□　□

A flaming fag sashays into the roughest truckstop on the highway, a parakeet on his shoulder. He looks around the restaurant at all the burly truckers and announces loudly, "Whichever one of you big bruisers can guess the weight of this darling parakeet gets to go home with me."

Silence falls over the truckstop. Then one of the toughest-looking guys speaks up. "That's an easy one—five hundred pounds."

The fag shrieks delightedly, "We have a winner! We have a winner!"

□   □   □

Two gay guys were talking when one leaned over and said to the other, "You know, I just got circumcised two weeks ago."

"How wonderful," gasped his friend. "You must let me see it."

The first man obliged, pulling down his pants and proudly displaying his cock.

"Ooooh!" shrieked his friend. "You look ten years younger!"

□   □   □

Know how you get hearing AIDS?

From listening to assholes.

□   □   □

Is it better to be born black or gay?

Black, because you don't have to tell your parents.

Cruelty To Animals

A man was surprised by the sight of a fellow walking down the sidewalk holding a three-legged pig on a leash. Unable to restrain his curiosity, he crossed the street and said to the guy, "That's quite a pig you have there."

"Let me tell you about this pig," said the guy. "This pig is the most amazing animal that ever lived. Why, one night my house caught on fire when my wife and I were out, and this pig carried my three children to safety and put out the fire before the firemen could get there."

"Wow!" said the first man. "But what about . . ."

"And that's not all," interrupted the guy. "My house was broken into when my wife and I were sound asleep, and this pig had the valuables back in place and the thief in a half Nelson before we got to the bottom of the stairs."

"That's pretty impressive," conceded his listener. "But how come . . ."

"And listen to this!" burst in the guy. "When I fell through some thin ice while skating, this pig dove in and pulled me out and safely to shore. This pig saved my life!"

"That's really great," said the first man, "but I have to know one thing. How come the pig only has three legs?"

"Hey listen," replied the proud owner, "a pig like this you can't eat all at once."

□   □   □

What can you do with a dog with no legs?
Take it for a drag.

□   □   □

So what do you call a dog with no legs?
Nothing. It can't come when you call.

□   □   □

Very concerned because his hens were laying fewer and fewer eggs each week, a farmer finally pinpointed the blame on his aging rooster, who clearly wasn't fulfilling his henhouse responsibilities. So he went out and bought a studly young rooster. Eyeing the newcomer, the old rooster said, "Listen, let's make a deal: I'll just take three hens, move over to that far corner, and leave all the rest to you."

"Not a chance," said the youngster. "This is my henhouse now and all the broads are mine."

"Very well," said the old rooster humbly, "but perhaps you'd do me one small favor to save my pride. Let's have a race and the winner gets the henhouse; that way it won't look as though I'm being replaced because I can't perform anymore."

Sizing up his rickety competitor, the young cock agreed, even granting him a four-length handicap. Off they started around the course, but it soon became evident that the four-length lead wasn't going to hold for long. Pretty soon it was down to two lengths, and as they rounded the turn, going flat out, the youngster was just about to overtake the old rooster. Just then the farmer stepped out onto his porch, grabbed his shotgun, and blasted the new bird into smithereens. "Dammit!" he said as he set the gun down, "That's the third gay rooster I've bought this month."

□   □   □

What goes "Hoppity . . . clank . . . hoppity . . . clank?"

The Easter Bunny with polio.

□   □   □

A Polish biology professor was conducting research on the nervous system of the frog. Taking a frog out of the tank and putting it on the table, he said, "Jump!" The frog jumped.

Taking a scalpel, he amputated one of the frog's front legs. "Jump!" he shouted. The frog jumped.

He amputated a hind leg. "Jump!" The frog managed a respectable jump.

Amputating a third limb, the professor repeated his command. Bleeding profusely by now, the frog managed a feeble bounce.

Taking his scalpel to the fourth leg, the professor said, "Jump!" No response from the frog. "I said *jump!*" shouted the professor. The frog didn't move. "JUMP!" he bellowed in the ear of the inert animal. No movement whatsoever, and finally the scientist gave up, considering the experiment at an end.

Taking his notebook from the shelf, the Polish scientist carefully noted, "When all limbs are amputated, it is observed that the frog goes deaf."

□ □ □

A farmer was extolling the virtues of pig fucking to his neighbor and urging him to give it a try. Finally, after hours of convincing, the neighbor agreed to mount one of his sows.

"I don't know Clem," the neighbor reported, "I didn't enjoy that too much."

"No wonder Clyde," the farmer laughed, "you picked the ugliest one!"

□ □ □

A man suspects his wife of cheating on him, so he goes to the pet store to shop for a parrot. He sees quite an assortment for sale for $500 to $1000, but that's a bit more than he wants to spend, so he's delighted to come across one in the corner for sale for $29.95. "How come that one's so cheap?" he asks the clerk.

"To tell ya the truth, his dick's oversized and embarrasses the customers" is the explanation. The husband buys the bird anyway, and installs it on a perch right over the bed.

The next day the first thing he does after coming home from work is to rush upstairs. "Well, what happened today?" he demands of the bird.

"Well, the milkman came, and . . . your wife told him to come into the bedroom, and . . . they took off their clothes, and . . . got into bed."

"So what happened next," screams the irate husband.

"I don't know," says the parrot. "I got hard and fell off my perch."

□ □ □

Mr. Johnson went out on his annual hunting expedition and actually succeeded in bagging a pheasant. He proudly brought it home and did his best to clean it, and that night the family sat down to a pheasant dinner. After a few mouthfuls his wife jumped up and ran for the bathroom. She came back a few minutes later and said, "Honey, there were little black things in my shit. What do you think it could be?"

"Uh-oh," said Mr. Johnson, "I guess I didn't clean the pheasant out too well. Just keep an eye out for the birdshot while you're eating."

About five minutes later his daughter dashed for the bathroom. She came out crying, "Daddy, Daddy, there's black things floating in my pee!"

"Pellets again—I'm really sorry. Don't worry, they won't hurt you," he reassured her.

Soon enough his son strolled off, coming back to the table ten minutes later. "What's wrong with you, Billy?" asked Mr. Johnson.

"I was jerking off and I shot the dog."

□ □ □

What do you do with a bird with no wings?
Take it for a spin.

□ □ □

Two guys were walking down the street when they came across a dog sitting on the sidewalk studiously licking its balls.

"Would I ever like to do that," sighed one man enviously.

"Go right ahead," encouraged his friend. "But if I were you, I'd pat him first."

□ □ □

The old rooster could never get enough. He screwed every chicken in the barnyard and wore them all out, so the farmer put him in with the ducks. Pretty soon all the ducks were begging for a rest, so the farmer tethered the rooster out in a cornfield. After a while the farmer looked out his window and saw that the bird was lying on the ground and looked dead as a doornail. Going out to check, he found the rooster lying down all right, but with its eyes wide open. "What's the matter?" he asked.

"*Shhhhh,*" hissed the rooster, motioning upward with the top of a wing. "Turkey vultures!"

□ □ □

There was once a Texan who had an unreasonable dislike of elephants. Realizing it bordered on a phobia, he consulted a psychiatrist who told him it was a fairly common problem. "The cure is straightforward," said the shrink. "You have to go to Africa and shoot one."

The idea appealed to the Texan so he flew to Kenya and hired a guide to take him on an elephant-hunting safari. The hunter's right-hand man turned out to be a native who in turn hired a bunch of his fellow tribesmen to spread out in a long line, beat drums and blow horns, and drive the elephants towards the blind where the hunters were waiting. As they waited, the noise grew louder and louder until out of the bush with much clanging and shouting burst the head beater. The Texan drew a bead and shot him right between the eyes.

"What the hell'd you do that for?" bellowed the guide. "He's my best beater—I've worked with him for twenty years!"

"If there's anything I hate worse than elephants," drawled the Texan, "it's big, noisy niggers."

□ □ □

Hearing a noise behind him, a streetcorner violinist turned around to see two dogs screwing in the alley. "Don't just stand there," growled one of them, "play 'Bolero.'"

□ □ □

Why do you wrap a hamster in electrician's tape?
So it won't explode when you fuck it.

□ □ □

A retired schoolteacher finally realized she was tired of living alone and wanted some companionship, so after a good deal of thought she decided to visit the local pet shop. The owner suggested a parrot, with which she could conduct a civilized conversation. This seemed an excellent idea, so she bought a handsome parrot, sat him on a perch in her living room, and said, "Say 'Pretty boy.'" Silence from the bird. "Come on, now, say 'Pretty boy . . . pretty boy.'"

At long last, disgustedly, the bird said, "Oh, shit."

Shocked, the schoolteacher said, "Just for that, you get five minutes in the refrigerator." Five minutes later she put the shivering bird back on its perch and said, "Now let's hear it: 'Pretty boy . . . pretty boy.'"

"Lay off for Christ's sake, would ya, lady?" said the parrot.

Outraged, the woman grabbed the bird, said, "That's it! Ten minutes in the freezer," and slammed the door on him.

Hopping about to keep warm, what did the parrot come across but a frozen turkey waiting for Thanksgiving. Startled, he squawked, "My God, you must have told the bitch to go fuck herself!"

□   □   □

What are the three reasons why sex is better with sheep?

They're always in the mood.

They never have a headache.

When you're through screwing them, you can eat them.

□   □   □

A young man was delighted to finally be asked home to meet the parents of the young woman he'd been seeing for some time. He was quite nervous about the meeting, though, and by the time he arrived punctually at the doorstep he was in a state of gastric distress. The problem developed into one of acute flatulence, and halfway through the canapés the young man realized he couldn't hold it in one second longer without exploding. A tiny fart escaped.

"Spot!" called out the young woman's mother to the family dog, lying at the young man's feet.

Relieved at the dog's having been blamed, the young man let another, slightly larger one go.

"Spot!" she called out sharply.

"I've got it made," thought the fellow to himself. One more and I'll feel fine. So he let loose a really big one.

"*Spot!*" shrieked the mother. "Get over here before he shits on you!"

Religion

*J*esus was making his usual rounds in heaven when he noticed a wizened, white-haired old man sitting in a corner looking very disconsolate. The next week he was disturbed to come across him again, looking equally miserable, and a week later he stopped to talk to him.

"See here, old fellow," said Jesus kindly, "this is heaven. The sun is shining, you've got all you could want to eat, all the instruments you might want to play—you're supposed to be blissfully happy! What's wrong?"

"Well," said the old man, "you see, I was a carpenter on earth, and lost my only, dearly beloved son at an early age. And here in heaven I was hoping more than anything to find him."

Tears sprang to Jesus' eyes. "Father!" he cried.

The old man jumped to his feet, bursting into tears, and sobbed, "Pinocchio!"

□   □   □

One day Father O'Malley was walking through the park when he came upon an enchanting scene. A beautiful little girl with long blond hair, deep blue eyes, and a dainty white lace dress was playing under a tree with her adorable little dog.

What a lovely picture, thought Father O'Malley to himself. Walking over, he asked, "Child, what is your name?"

"Blossom," she replied.

"What a fitting name," exclaimed Father O'Malley. "And how did your parents come to choose such a pretty name?"

"Well, one day when I was still in my mommie's tummy she was lying under this very tree when a blossom fell and landed on her stomach. She thought it was a message from God and decided that if I were a girl, my name would be Blossom," explained the little girl sweetly.

How charming, thought the priest. He started to walk away, then turned back. "And the name of your little dog?" he inquired.

"Porky," was the child's reply.

Again he asked her how the unusual name had been chosen.

"Because he likes to fuck pigs."

□ □ □

An ambitious new sales rep for Budweiser beer traveled all the way to Rome and managed to finagle an audience with the Pope himself. As soon as the two were alone together, he leaned over and whispered, "Your Holiness, I have an offer I think might interest you. I'm in a position to give you a million dollars if you'll change the wording in the Lord's Prayer to 'our daily beer.' Now whaddaya say?"

"Absolutely not," said the shocked Pontiff.

"Hey, I understand; it's a big decision," sympathized the salesman. "How about five million dollars?"

"I couldn't think of it," sputtered the Pope.

"I know it's a tough one. Tell you what—I can go up to fifty million dollars," proposed the salesman.

Asking him to leave the room, the Pope called in the Cardinal and whispered, "When does our contract with Pillsbury expire?"

□   □   □

Jesus, Moses, and an old man are playing golf. Moses tees up and hits his ball into the water trap. Nonplussed, he goes over to the lake, parts the water with his club, and hits his ball onto the green.

Jesus tees up next, and also manages to land in the water trap. So he walks down to the lake, across the water, and hits his ball out onto the green.

Last to tee up is the old man, whose ball heads straight for the water. As the ball hits the surface a fish jumps up and swallows it but is immediately grabbed by an eagle, which deposits the fish on the green. The ball shoots out of the fish's mouth and rolls into the cup.

Jesus turns around and says, "Nice shot, Dad, but would you quit fucking around and play golf?"

□   □   □

A rabbi, a priest, and a minister were having a discussion as to how they divided up the collection plate. The minister explained that he drew a circle on the ground, tossed the collection in the air, and that all the money that landed in the circle was for God and all that landed outside was for himself and the parish. The priest said that his system was similar: He just drew a straight line, tossed the money up, and that what landed on one side was for God and on the other for himself and the church. The rabbi admitted that his system worked along somewhat the same lines. "I just toss the plate up in the air," he explained, "and anything God can catch he can keep."

□   □   □

It's the eve of Pontius Pilate's birthday and his guards are sitting around trying to figure out something really special for the event. Finally they hit on a great idea: they'll nail all the Jews in the land up on crosses and use them to line the road to Pilate's house.

The next morning all the guards crowd around Pilate to wish him happy birthday and urge him to come outside. When he does, he's amazed and touched by the spectacle and begins to stroll down the road. At the very end he notices Jesus, King of the Jews. Unlike the rest, Jesus is still conscious and appears to be mumbling something, so since the King of the Jews might be saying something important, Pilate commands a ladder to be leaned up against the cross.

Climbing up and putting his ear to Jesus's lips, Pilate hears him mumbling, "Happy birthday to you, happy birthday to you . . ."

□   □   □

When the Eisenbergs moved to Rome little Jaime came home from school in tears. He explained to his mother that the nuns were always asking these Catholic questions and how was he, a nice Jewish boy, supposed to know the answers?

Mrs. Eisenberg's heart swelled with maternal sympathy and she determined to help her son out. "Jaime," she said, "I'm going to embroider the answers on the inside of your shirt and you just look down and read them the next time those nuns pick on you."

"Thanks, Mom," said Jaime, and he didn't bat an eye when Sister Michael asked him who the world's most famous virgin was. "Mary," he answered.

"Very good," said the nun. "And who was her husband?"

"Joseph," answered the boy.

"I see you've been studying. Now can you tell me the name of their son?"

"Sure," said Jaime. "Calvin Klein."

□　□　□

A priest, a minister, and a rabbi are all enjoying a beer together when a fly lands right in the priest's glass. Fishing it out, the priest shakes off the fly and throws it in the air, saying, "Be on your way, little creature."

Five minutes later the fly is back, this time making a nosedive for the minister's beer. Fishing it out and shaking it dry, the minister tosses it in the air, saying, "Be free, little bug."

But the fly is a slow learner and ends up five minutes later in the rabbi's glass. Picking it up and shaking it violently, the rabbi screams, "Spit it out, spit it out!"

□　□　□

One day not too long ago, God decided He was overdue for a vacation. "I hear Mars is nice," suggested St. Peter.

"Not again," said God. "I'm still sore from the sunburn I got there 10,000 years ago."

"I had a good time on Pluto," piped up the Archangel Gabriel.

"No way," said God. "I nearly broke my neck 5,000 years ago skiing there."

"There's always Earth," spoke up a small seraph.

"Are you nuts?" shouted God. "I dropped by there 2,000 years ago and I'm still in trouble for knocking up some Jewish chick."

□ □ □

Christ is on the cross, and Peter is down the hill comforting Mary Magdalene when he hears in a faint voice, "Peter . . . Peter . . ."

"I must go and help my Savior," he said and went up the hill, only to be beaten and kicked back down by the Roman centurions guarding the cross. But soon he hears, "Peter . . . Peter" in even fainter tones, and he cannot ignore the call. Peter limps up the hill, leans a ladder against the cross, and is halfway up when the centurions knock over the ladder, beat him brutally, and toss him back down the hill.

Again he hears, "Peter . . . Peter . . ." ever fainter, and he cannot sit idle. He staggers up the hill, drags himself up the ladder, and finally gets even with Christ's face. Just as the centurions are reaching for the ladder, Christ says, "Peter . . . Peter . . . I can see your house from here."

□ □ □

What's the difference between Jesus Christ and an oil painting?

You only need one nail to hang up a painting.

Begin invited the Pope to play golf. Since the Pope had no idea how to play, he convened the College of Cardinals to ask their advice. "Call Jack Nicklaus," they suggested, "and let him play in your place. Tell Begin you're sick or something."

Honored by His Holiness's request, Nicklaus agreed to represent him on the links. John Paul, again with advice from his staff, made him a cardinal just in case Begin were to get suspicious.

When Nicklaus returned from the match, the Pope asked him how he had done. "I came in second," was the reply.

"You mean to tell me Begin beat you?" John Paul yelled.

"No, Your Holiness," said Jack. "Rabbi Palmer did."

Old Age

*A*n eager-beaver young real estate agent was doing his best to sell this old coot a condominium in Palm Beach. Having outlined its many attractions in detail, he confidently concluded his pitch: "And, Mr. Rosenblatt, this is an investment in the future."

"Sonny," croaked Mr. Rosenblatt, "at my age I don't even buy green bananas."

□   □   □

Two old guys wonder if there's baseball in heaven and promise each other that the first to get there will somehow let the other know. A week later one of them dies. A week after that he contacts his friend on earth and says, "Joe, I've got some good news and some bad news. The good news is that there *is* a baseball team in heaven. The bad news is that you're pitching on Friday."

□   □   □

"Doctor," an old man complained, "I can't pee."

"Hmmm," contemplated the doctor, "How old are you?"

"Eighty-seven" the old man replied.
"Well, haven't you peed enough?"

□   □   □

The girls in the whorehouse were frankly sceptical
when a ninety-year-old man came in and put his money
down on the front desk, but finally a good-hearted
hooker took him up to her room. Imagine her surprise
when he proceeded to make love to her with more en-
ergy and skill than any man she had ever known. "I've
never come so many times," she gasped. "How about
once more, on the house?"

"All right," conceded the old geezer, "but I have to
take a five-minute nap and you must keep your hands
on my penis, just so, while I'm asleep." She agreed eagerly, and as soon as he woke up he gave her an even
better lesson in lovemaking.

"Oh, God," gasped the hooker ecstatically, "I can't
get enough of you. Please, just once more—I'll pay
you."

The old man agreed, subject to the same condi-
tions, and just before he nodded out, the hooker said,
"Excuse me, but would you mind explaining about the
nap and why I have to keep my hands on your pri-
vates?"

"I'm ninety years old," retorts the man, "so is it so
surprising I need a little rest? As for the other, it's because the last time while I was napping, they took my
wallet."

□   □   □

At his annual checkup Bernie was given an excellent bill
of health. "It must run in your family," commented the
doctor. "How old was your dad when he died?"

"What makes you think he's dead?" asked Bernie.

"He's ninety and going strong."

"Aha! And how long did your grandfather live?"

"What makes you think he's dead, doc? He's a hundred and ten years old and getting married to a twenty-two-year-old in two weeks," retorted Bernie.

"At his age!" exclaimed the doc. "Why's he want to get married to a twenty-two-year-old?"

"Doc," said Bernie, "what makes you think he *wants* to?"

□ □ □

Sam and Sally were virgins when they were married and so embarrassed about the sex act that they agreed to refer to it as "doing the laundry." Fifty years later their prudery had not diminished, but every so often Sam would get his hopes up and ask if he could put something in the washing machine. "Maybe in a little while, Sam," Sally answered one cold night as they tottered into the bedroom.

Under the covers he poked her in the ribs and asked, "How about a little laundry, honey?"

No answer from Sally, but about ten minutes later, having thought it over, she whispered, "Okay, Sam, the washing machine's ready."

"Aw, gee, honey," he quavered, "it was just a small load, I did it by hand."

□ □ □

Milton was getting on in years—he was well into his eighties—and decided it was time for a last fling. So he went out and hired himself a prostitute for a last night of pleasure.

About three weeks later he felt a growing pain in

his groin and rushed over to the doctor's office, insisting on an emergency consultation. The doctor examined him thoroughly, then asked if he could ask a personal question.

"Have you been with a woman anytime recently?"

Milton confessed the truth.

"Well, you better go look her up right away, 'cause you're about to come!"

□ □ □

Whitney woke up in the middle of the night and cried until his mother came in to see what was the matter. "I have to make pee pee," wailed the little boy.

"All right," said his mother. "I'll take you to the bathroom."

"No," insisted Whitney, "I want Grandma."

"Don't be silly, I can do the same thing as Grandma," said his mother firmly."

"Uh-uh. Her hands shake."

Miscellaneous

A lovelorn young man wrote to an advice columnist as follows:

Dear Abby,

I just met the most terrific girl and we get along fabulously. I think she's the one for me. There's just one problem: I can't remember from our first date if she told me she had T.B. or V.D. What should I do?
—Confused

Abby replies:

Dear Confused,

If she coughs, fuck her.

□   □   □

It's after dinner when this guy realizes he's out of cigarettes. He decides to pop down to the corner bar for a pack, telling his wife he'll be right back. The bartender offers him a draft on the house and he decides he has time for just one. He's nursing it along when a gorgeous blonde comes in the door, but he looks the other way because he knows he has no time to fool around. So can he help it if she comes and sits right next to him and says how thirsty she is?

One thing leads to another and eventually the girl says how much she likes him and invites him back to her apartment to get better acquainted. How can he refuse? They go back to her place and go at it like crazy, and the next thing he knows it's four o'clock in the morning. Jumping out of bed, the guy shakes the girl awake and asks if she has any baby powder.

"Yeah, in the bathroom cabinet," she says groggily.

He dusts his hands liberally with the powder, drives home at 90 mph, and pulls into the driveway to find his wife waiting up for him with a rolling pin in her hand. "So where've you been?" she screeches.

"Well, you see, honey," he stammers, "I only went out for cigarettes, but Jake offered me a beer and then this beautiful bombshell walked in and we got to talking and drinking and we've been back at her apartment fucking like bunnies . . ."

"Wait a minute," snaps his wife. "Let me see your hands." Turning on him furiously, she says, "Don't you *ever* try lying to me again, you rotten little skunk— you've been bowling again!"

□　□　□

A cowboy traveling across the desert came across a lovely woman, naked and battered, her limbs tied to four stakes in the ground.

"Thank God you've come!" she cried. "I was on my way to San Francisco when a whole tribe of Indians attacked our wagon train. They stole our food, kidnapped our children, torched our wagons . . . and raped me over and over."

"Lady," said the cowboy as he unbuckled his belt, "today just ain't your day."

□   □   □

It's late at night when a spaceship lands in the middle of nowhere in central Iowa. The Martians—who look kind of like your average gas pump, not exactly but pretty close—descend from the ship and begin looking for signs of intelligent life. Coming across a road they follow it until they come across a one-pump gas station, which looks somewhat like a Martian—not exactly, but pretty close.

The captain is overjoyed—this must be what they are seeking! Deciding to make contact, he intones to the pumps, "Greetings. We come from planet Xjbzoldt in search of intelligent beings. Will you take us to your leader?" When there's no response, he repeats his query as loudly as possible. Still no answer, so he turns to his voice translator. Finally, enraged by the lack of a reply, he whips out his laser gun and points it at the pump. "Why, you insolent son of a whore—take us to your leader or I'll blast you!" His lieutenant tries to stop him, but it's too late. The captain fires, and an immense explosion hurls the Martians a hundred feet in the air.

Three hours later they're coming to, the lieutenant helping the captain to his feet. In a shaky voice the captain asks, "Wha . . . what happened?

The lieutenant replies, "Look, Captain, if I told you once, I told you a hundred times: you just don't go messing with a guy who can wrap his prick twice around his waist and stick it in his ear."

Little Mortie got a real surprise when he barged into his parents' room one night. "And you slap me for sucking my *thumb!*" he screamed.

□ □ □

A woman went into the neighborhood grocery store and asked the grocer for a can of cat food. Knowing that she didn't have a cat, the grocer asked why she was buying the stuff. "It's for my husband's lunch," was the answer.

Shocked, the grocer said, "You can't feed cat food to your husband. It'll kill him!"

"I've been giving it to him for a week now and he likes it fine," was her answer, and each day the woman continued to come in and purchase a can of cat food for her husband's lunch.

It wasn't too much later that the grocer happened to be scanning the obituary column in the local paper and noticed that the woman's husband has passed away. When the woman came into the store he couldn't resist saying, "I'm sorry to hear about your husband, but I warned you that he'd die if you kept feeding him cat food."

"It wasn't the cat food that killed him," she retorted. "He broke his neck trying to lick his ass!"

□ □ □

A settler in the Midwest felt he had to protect his family from wild animals and unfriendly Indians—but he also needed to chop wood for the fire. So he bought a large bell and set it up outside, instructing his wife to ring it in case of an emergency.

The next day he was busy chopping wood when he

heard the bell ring in the distance. Terrified, he grabbed his rifle and ran home, only to find his wife standing in the clearing holding a tray. "I baked you some cookies, honey," she said.

Patiently he explained that the bell was only for a real emergency, and went back to chopping wood. Just a few days later the bell rang again and he rushed back, only to be shown a wounded bird his son had brought home. This, he made clear a little less patiently, was not his idea of a dangerous emergency.

A week later he rushed home at the clang of the bell. Reaching the clearing, he found that the house had been felled by a tornado, his wife had been murdered and scalped by Indians, and wildcats were gnawing the bloody remains of his children.

"Now, this is more like it!" said the settler.

□ □ □

What's the difference between love and herpes?
Herpes is forever.

□ □ □

A prosperous stockbroker and his wife had everything money could buy, until the broker gambled on a few bad tips and lost everything. He came home with a heavy heart that night and said to his wife, "You better learn to cook, Myrna, so we can fire the cook."

His wife thought it over for a few moments and said, "Okay, but you better learn to screw, George, so we can fire the chauffeur."

There was once a salesman who had an outstanding record for selling toothbrushes. His boss, wondering at this unlikely success, sent a man out to follow the salesman on rounds to see what pitch he gave that brought such good results. It was soon found that this particular salesman went to the corner of a busy street and opened up his briefcase, and on one side was the assortment of toothbrushes, and on the other side a bag of potato chips and a small bowl of brownish stuff. He would grab a likely customer and give them the following pitch.

"Good morning, ma'am, this is a commercial promotion for —————— brand of chip dip. Would you care to give it a try?" At that point the person would try it, then spit it out and scream in utter disgust. "This tastes like shit!" The salesman would smile and say, "It is. You want to buy a toothbrush?"

□   □   □

What's the definition of an anchovy?
A small fish that smells like a finger.

□   □   □

Deciding it was time for a history review, the teacher asked the class, "Who can tell me what historical figure said, 'I have not yet begun to fight'?"

The little Japanese girl in the front row raised her hand and answered, "John Paul Jones."

"Very good, Miyako. Now, who can tell me who said, 'I regret that I have but one life to give for my country?'"

Again the little Japanese girl was the only one to raise her hand, and piped up, "That's Nathan Hale."

The teacher said to the class, "What's going on? So far Miyako's the only one to answer any of my questions."

Suddenly a voice was heard from the back of the room. "Aw, fuck the Japanese!"

"Who said that?" asked the teacher sharply.

Miyako's hand shot up. "Lee Iacocca!" she said brightly.

□ □ □

An attorney was defending his client against a charge of first-degree murder. "Your Honor, my client is accused of stuffing his lover's mutilated body into a suitcase and heading for the Mexican border. Just north of Tijuana a cop spotted her hand sticking out of the suitcase.

"Now, I would like to stress that my client is *not* a murderer. A sloppy packer, maybe . . ."

□ □ □

A middle-aged man confided to his doctor that he was tired of his wife and wished there were some way of doing her in so that he could have some good years left to himself. "Screw her every day for a year," counseled the doctor. "She'll never make it."

As chance would have it, it was about a year later when the doctor happened to drop by his patient's house. On the porch sat the husband looking frail and thin; tan and robust, his wife could be seen out back splitting wood."

"Say, Sam, you're looking good," said the doctor uneasily, "and Laura certainly's the picture of health."

"Little does she know," hissed Sam with a wicked little smile, "she dies tomorrow."

□   □   □

There was a wealthy old gentleman who desired the services of a prostitute, so he arranged with a call-girl service to send over their $1000, top-of-the-line girl. She got all dolled up, rode over to his fancy apartment building, and was escorted up to his penthouse, where the door was opened by the elderly millionaire himself. "And what can I do for you tonight, sir?" she asked in her throatiest voice, dropping her fur coat to reveal a slinky lamé dress.

"Hot tub," he said.

So they went into his luxuriously appointed bathroom where she settled him into the tub. "And now, sir?" she asked.

"Waves," he said.

So she perched herself on the edge of the tub and proceeded to kick her feet vigorously to make waves. "And *next*, sir?"

"Thunder."

Obligingly banging her hand against the side of the tub, she felt it necessary to remind him that he was paying $1000 for her special services, and surely there was some sort of special service she could perform for him.

"Yes," he said, "lightning."

Kicking her feet in the water, banging on the side of the tub with one hand, and flicking the light switch on and off with the other, she felt obliged to give it one more shot. "Sir, you know I am a hooker . . . Uh, sexual matters are my specialty . . . Isn't there something along those lines you'd be interested in?"

"In *this* weather?" he said, looking up at her. "Are you crazy?"

□ □ □

A young country girl came to town for a day. She was window-shopping when a beautiful pair of red shoes caught her eye, and as she stood admiring them the clerk came out and asked if he could help her. The girl admitted that she'd spent all her money but that she'd do anything to get her hands on those red shoes.

The clerk thought it over for a moment. "I think we can work out a deal," he told her. "Go lie down on the couch in the back room." Soon he came in and closed the door. "So do you want those shoes bad enough to put out for them?" he asked. When she nodded he pulled down his pants, exposing a hard-on about nine inches long. "Honey, I'll screw with this big cock of mine until you squirm with pleasure and scream in ecstasy and go wild with desire."

"I don't get much of a kick out of sex, but go right ahead," said the girl, spreading her legs and lying back. Sure she couldn't last long, the salesman started pumping away, but she lay there like a dishrag. Pretty soon he'd come twice and began to worry about getting soft, so he started going at it for all he was worth. Sure enough he felt her arms go around his neck and her legs tighten around his waist. "Best fuck you've ever had, right?" chortled the man. In a couple of seconds you'll be coming like crazy."

"Oh, no, it's not that," said the girl. "I'm just trying on my new shoes."

□ □ □

A young guy had gone to his doctor for a routine checkup, and when he came in for the results, the doctor said gravely, "Jerry, I think you'd better sit down. I've got some good news and some bad news."

"Okay, Doc," said Jerry. "Give me the bad news first."

"Well," said the doctor, "you've got cancer. It's spreading at an unbelievably rapid rate, it's totally inoperable, and you've got about three weeks to live."

"Jesus," said Jerry, wiping a bead of sweat off his brow. "What's the *good* news?"

"You know that really cute receptionist out in the front office?"

"You bet!" said Jerry.

"The one with the big tits and the cute little ass?"

"Right!"

"And the long blond hair?"

"Yeah, yeah," said Jerry impatiently.

"Well," said the doctor, leaning forward with a smile, "I'm fucking her!"

Too Tasteless To Be Included

Why do blacks smell?
So blind people can hate them too.

□   □   □

The victim of an awful automobile accident was pronounced dead on arrival at the hospital, and the emergency-room nurse was instructed to prepare the body for the undertaker. Removing his bloody clothes, she discovered that the young man had died with the most massive erection she had ever seen. Unable to take her eyes off it, she finally yielded to temptation, took off her panties, straddled the stiff, and proceeded to enjoy herself. She was getting down from the table when a second nurse came in and reprimanded her for her obscene behavior. "What's the harm?" shot back the first nurse. "I enjoyed it, and he surely didn't mind it. Besides, he can't complain and I can't get pregnant. Why don't you give it a try."

"Oh, I couldn't possibly," said the second nurse, blushing. "First, he's dead, and second, I've got my period. Listen, the doctor wants you in the operating room, and I'm supposed to finish up in here." She got to work, but soon found herself terribly excited by this massive hard-on and climbed on top of it. Just as she was starting to come, she was astonished to feel the man climax too. Looking down and seeing his eyelids starting to flutter, she exclaimed, "I thought you were dead!"

"I thought I was, too, lady," said the man, "until you gave me that blood transfusion."

□　□　□

What's the difference between Baby Fae's death and the death of the baboon?
The baboon's death wasn't funny.

□　□　□

This little boy about ten years old walks into a whorehouse dragging a dead frog on a string behind him. Walking up to the madam, he says, "I would like a girl for the evening."

"I'm sorry, but I can't help you. You're too young," says the madam.

The little boy takes $200 out of his wallet and hands it over. "One lady, coming right up," she says.

"One condition," says the little boy. "The lady has to have active herpes."

"I'm sorry, but I can't help you. All my girls are clean," says the madam.

The little boy takes another $200 out of his wallet and she says, "One dirty lady, coming right up." So the little boy goes upstairs with the prostitute. About twenty-five minutes later the boy comes downstairs all happy and smiling, still dragging his dead frog behind him. As he heads out the door, the madam says, "May I ask you a question? Why did you insist on a woman with herpes."

"It goes like this," says the little boy. "When I get home tonight, my babysitter will be there. I'll make love with her and she'll get the herpes. When my parents get back my dad will drive the babysitter home, screw the babysitter, and catch the herpes. When he comes in, he'll make love with my mom and she'll catch it. Tomorrow morning about 8:00 my father will leave for work. At about 10:00 the milkman gets there, and he's the bastard who killed my FROG. . . ."

□   □   □

What's the difference between a dead dog in the road and a dead black in the road?

There's skid marks in front of the dog.

□   □   □

A newlywed couple check into a quiet, out-of-the-way lakeside hotel. The clerk and the bellhop tip broad winks at each other, smiling in anticipation of the honeymoon antics to come. But lo and behold, in the middle of the night (their first) who but the groom tromps down the stairs fully laden with fishing gear! This happens again on the second and third nights. The clerk and bellhop can contain their curiosity no longer:

"You're *fishing* in the middle of the night on your honeymoon? Why aren't you up making love to your wife?"

The groom looked bewildered. "Make love to her? Oh no, she's got gonorrhea."

Embarrassed silence. "Oh. What about anal sex?"

"Oh no, she's got diarrhea."

"I see. Well, there's oral sex. . . ."

"Oh no. She's got pyorrhea as well."

"Gonorrhea, diarrhea, *and* pyorrhea! Why, may I ask, did you marry her?"

"Because she's got worms—and I just *love* to fish."

□   □   □

Why does Helen Keller wear skin-tight pants?
So that people can read her lips.

□   □   □

Define BLIND SPOT.
What Dick and Jane do to be cruel.